D0890023

RESTORED

SURVIVING TO LIVE

A TRUE STORY BY

STEVEN ACOSTA, MD

NEWMAN SPRINGS PUBLISHING
320 Broad Street
Red Bank, NJ 07701

First originally published by Newman Springs Publishing 2021

ISBN 978-1-63881-306-4 (Paperback)
ISBN 978-1-63881-903-5 (Hardcover)
ISBN 978-1-63881-307-1 (Digital)

Printed in the United States of America

CONTENTS

FOREWORD

June 21, 2020, was a day that not only changed Steve forever but our entire family! *Restored* is the story of Steve's strength and perseverance to overcome huge challenges and come out even better than before. I could not be more proud of the man he has become in this process. His role changed in the hospital and at home, and he handled it gracefully and humbly while continuing to be our protector and leader. God restored my husband, our family, and our marriage through this awful situation. I hope that through this book, you will get a glimpse of the man I love and his ability to overcome gives you hope!

—Jan Acosta

My brother and sister, Luke and Annalise, were at home with my dad when the events in this book unfolded. I was a plane ride away, in the middle of the COVID pandemic. The fear that grew in the hours that it took me to get home now seem so small in comparison to the gratitude I have for where we are now as a family. It is hard to process how much has happened in just one year and even harder to imagine everything our dad has been through. I am thankful that he decided to share his experience, and I hope it reassures others who have loved ones in the ICU that their spirit can feel the love and concern they have. Even more special is that even my father, someone who has cared for countless critical patients, could not have predicted what he would go through—mind, body, or spirit. I find it sobering that even our advanced sciences cannot fully understand these things and humbling that God has called people, like our family, to serve others through health care. There is no secret to being restored. It does not magically make the days easier or the pain less. However, what it has given us is a lens of gratitude and a reinforcement in our faith that cannot be replicated (nor would I want it too). So if nothing else, I hope the sharing of this story fills you with gratitude and restores your faith.

—Shelby Acosta

CHAPTER 1

WAKING UP

The first memory I have of my hospital stay is waking up to see my ICU nurse Josh standing in the room in front of me. "Hello, Doc!" he said in his very kind and warm voice. "How are you feeling?"

I was feeling groggy and had an overwhelming sense of wanting to sleep. I was completely clueless what had transpired over the previous four to five days.

"Doc, you had a heart attack. You coded, but we got you back, and now you're all good!" Josh said by way of trying to orient me.

"I remember coming in to the ER with chest pain," I mustered.

"Yes, you went to the cath lab and got a new stent in your LAD. You're all good now. This is hospital day five," Josh shared.

"Where is Jan?" I asked, wondering where my wife and family were. In the era of COVID, there was limited, if any visitation, and given I had been in a coma for five days, I was still not fully aware of my surroundings or circumstance.

"Would you like me to call her?" Josh asked.

"Yes, do you mind?" I replied. While I was still coming awake, I had a sense that I desperately needed to see my wife, Jan. As soon as I heard Josh say she was on her way, I was anxious for her to arrive. I had no idea what time of day it was, but for whatever reason, I had a sense it might be early afternoon. I was scared and needed some semblance of home, a feeling of normal to calm the growing anxiety inside. Holy shit, what happened to me?

After some time passed, I continued to try to get my bearings and process what I had been told about the events that landed me in the hospital. I heard a familiar voice in the hallway. I was filled with excitement and some measure of relief. Jan was here. I waited expectantly as I anticipated her walking in at any minute. But I was mistaken, or my senses were off. I don't know, but that wasn't her voice I had heard.

After what seemed to be a half hour or so, I was finally relieved to see Jan coming through the doorway; she gave me a full and warm embrace. It was the first time she had been allowed to see me in person since the day I arrived in the emergency room. The last image she had of me was being intubated, swollen faced due to the compressions and increased pressure in my chest. Now, I was awake and talking. I sensed that she was evaluating me, determining if I was me again. I, of course, had no idea what she had been through or even the magnitude of what I had been through, but I knew I needed to let her know I was okay. "I'm okay, babe!" I shared.

She was strong and was not there to shed tears; she was there to be the rock I needed and to continue to be the rock she had been for everyone over the past week. I wasn't lying to her; I truly felt okay.

As we talked, it was apparent I wasn't quite myself. I was overwhelmingly tired, a strong feeling of fatigue where even changing positions in bed would make me feel the need for a nap. I also wasn't fully oriented to what day it was or how long I had been in the hospital to this point. I had no idea how sick I had been or how sick I was now.

We FaceTimed the kids so I could say hello. It was nice to finally see them and talk to them. Again, I was unaware of how much they had suffered emotionally and how their past few days had been filled with the fear and anxiety of not knowing how this would all turn out. For me, seeing them all together and safe was what I needed for now. God knows how much I needed to be reassured they were all safe.

Slowly, over the next few days, with Jan by my side as much as she was allowed, I regained strength; my mind became clearer. I was becoming me again. My appetite stirred just a little, and I asked for more food yet hadn't eaten what was given to me. Even when tempted by grape slushes or Keva Juice, I couldn't get the gel and metallic taste out of my mouth. It seemed to coat every bite I took no matter what I tried to eat. I'm sure it was the result of having been intubated. Doctors often use some gel on the instrument that is placed deep in the throat, the laryngoscope or nowadays, a video enabled GlideScope, which allows visualization of the area in which the breathing tube, called an endotracheal tube, is placed. That tube itself, of course, is some type of flexible plastic.

The ICU nurses were all phenomenal. Besides Josh, there was Ryan, who was still training. He had gone into nursing after a stint as a minor-league baseball pitcher. He was a tall, thin athletic kid. He enjoyed talking and would come in to check on me and end up staying and chatting for a bit. Conversation was taxing for me, but it was nice to talk about things other than how I was feeling. Julie took care of me initially, although I don't remember her much as she was my initial nurse and was my guardian during those initial critical hours after the cath lab. I was told of the amazing job she did. There was Adrianna, who was very detail oriented and supersharp. She had relayed to me some detail of the day I came into the emergency room; she had responded to the code blue call. She had prayed. She shared stories of taking her daughter out to a duck pond and saving a duck from being attacked by other ducks. Again, some conversation that was outside the normal line of questions regarding any symptoms I might or might not be having was nice. The respiratory therapists were all great. I had worked with all of them before. Rosie checked on me often and was always bright and positive.

They checked on me often, they treated me like any other patient but also maintained some level of professional courtesy for me, asking me about medication preferences, especially for sleep, not that any of my suggestions worked. They also allowed Jan in to help with things like sponge baths and walks to the bathroom. It was an adjustment, but I was allowed some level of privacy.

The physical therapists stopped by and began light therapy, the usual range of motion exercises, strengthening. I found standing up difficult at first; it was amazing how quickly I had weakened. It reminded me of standing up after twisting your ankle in a basketball game. You put pressure on your feet, but you're not sure if you're going to be able to hold yourself up. Standing up also felt odd, I would get a little light-headed and had the sensation of not fully being able to trust the strength in my legs. The primary concern, of course, being that I might fall.

Jan, much later, shared with me that I had demanded crutches from some of the staff, going so far as to say, "Just bring me some crutches, motherfucker." Gosh, those poor nurses and therapists. Knowing how it felt to be on the receiving end of a demanding and unreasonable patient request myself made me feel even worse when I heard stories about me acting like this. I hope they understood I wasn't myself.

I was on potent medication to keep my blood thin—triple therapy as we referred to it in medicine. While it kept the oxygen-carrying blood flowing easily through my newly treated coronary blood vessels, the medication also kept my blood from clotting. Any fall or even light trauma was cause for concern. Heck, it sometimes didn't even take trauma. I took care of a number of patients along the way, who unknowingly had gastrointestinal inflammation or ulcers, who developed life-threatening bleeding after initiating this type of medication. I kept my fingers crossed nothing of the sort would happen to me.

After a couple of days, I managed to regain some strength and walk with assistance. I felt my mind was sharpening but still had some fog and confusion intermittently. I rarely slept. There was a fair amount of anxiety about closing my eyes. When I did try, my mind would start to go over how bad things must've been when I arrived and the pain I still had in my chest, likely from the remarkable and heroic efforts of my colleagues as they worked tirelessly to save me. They worked and fought against even reason to make sure I survived. Although I did not suffer any fractured ribs from the extended time of chest compressions, they had left their mark; my chest hurt! If I allowed myself to even start to think about how sick I had been, how sick I was, how lucky I was to be here, sleep would never come.

As I gained strength, I had a couple of visitors, all doctors and advanced practice providers, with whom I worked closely in the very same hospital in which I was currently a patient. There were no visitors allowed at this time, but the nurses looked the other way since it was well-wishing providers coming by. Besides, how often do doctors ever follow the rules? They were all very kind; all wished me well and talked of their own fears that had been stirred up with my seemingly out-of-the-blue medical event. A couple of them confessed to going to their own doctors for checkups. I had scared everyone, and everyone felt vulnerable, as the stress of work, the stress of a pandemic clearly took its toll on everyone.

As has been well-documented, being a patient in the time of COVID brings challenges with regard to keeping families informed. Initially, no one was allowed to see me in the ICU while I was intubated and had an Impella device in place, helping my heart pump blood to my body because my heart was initially too weak to do it on its own. My ICU nurse and the ICU nurse manager would take it upon themselves to make time to FaceTime Jan and the kids and allow them to see me and talk to me, even though I was sedated. Jan and the kids encouraged me through the screen and said prayers aloud. The remarkable nurses would also direct Jan and the kids *outside* the ICU wing of the hospital and show them which my window was. They would come to see me for themselves, peering through my window and praying for my survival. They were an amazing prayer team. The kindness and caring nature of my nurses can't be overstated. They were simply amazing to me and my family.

After I woke up and was extubated, Jan was allowed to sneak in and see me and stay for a few minutes at a time. If my nurse was tied up and not able to keep track of when Jan arrived, we took advantage, and Jan would stay for hours; it was a remarkable comfort to me. I desperately wanted my kids to know I was okay, so we would FaceTime for a period and let them see that I was awake and getting better every day.

I know they must've been so frightened. I can't imagine the acute jolt it was to their lives. I was the middle-aged dad who played up the fact that I was Superman. I ran around our neighborhood for exercise; I mowed the lawn; I washed the cars; I took the dog for walks; I learned to fly planes and earned a private pilot's license;

I worked two jobs and would often do double shifts in the urgent care, where I was medical director and in the same emergency room where I was ultimately resuscitated by my colleagues. I drank beer and played golf with my brother and friends. I drank good wine and had great nights of conversation with my wife. I took my family on great trips, and we would sit around a great dinner table sharing laughs and making new memories. Simply put, I was living life, and I was on the go!

Now, I was the complete opposite. I was sick; I had just enough strength to walk to the bathroom. I was dependent on others for help, and I was intermittently confused. The future seemed bleak, but we were all glad there would be a future to experience.

CHAPTER 2

THE SETUP

The time prior to the day I arrived in the emergency room was very stressful and challenging. In January, we had traveled to southern California for a PGA Tour event, the Farmers Open. We were excited to go with our friends Jeremiah and Veronica. Jeremiah was a Farmers agent who had offered to get us passes. We were accidentally dropped off in the player arrival area and got to see our PGA tour heroes up close. It was a great day and a great time.

Like the rest of the world, we woke up on that Sunday to the horrible news of Kobe Bryant's helicopter accident. We were completed deflated by the news. We also noted news of a virus outbreak in China. We noticed some of our Uber drivers were wearing masks. Odd, we thought.

As the months passed, we were overwhelmed by the remarkably quick changes in the outbreak of the virus to include newly infected patients being identified in various countries; there was talk of halting travel, closing businesses. It was all so surreal. Then the days came; the country was shutting down. Only critical businesses would be required to be open. Of course, that meant as an ER doc, I would continue working and being prepared the anticipated local outbreak. We met and rehearsed the tasks of donning protective gear. We got our N95 masks updated. It was a scary time.

As with most of the world, significant changes were in place at work due to the pandemic. I had decided to leave my urgent care medical director's position in order to move over full time into the emergency room. I had been asked to become the director of the ER by the regional medical director, who was serving in that role temporarily until a new director could be found. I had been apprehensive about making such a dramatic move, but the pay increase would be significant, and it would allow me to work fewer clinical days per month. After some deliberation with Jan, I decided to jump in.

I was told I would simply join the full-time staff in the ER initially as it was March, and with the changes implemented due to the ongoing pandemic, the regional medical director indicated it was best to not make any significant changes at this time, but in two to three months, we would have me transition into the position. It seemed odd to me, but given the things going on in the world, it was an odd time. Interestingly, in spite of the start of the pandemic, things actually slowed down in our ER. Like many places that were not yet facing a surge in cases, we actually experienced a significant slowdown in terms of patient volume. This led to multiple changes in our group, including a cut in pay and decreased support from advance practice providers during the day. Many of the APPs were furloughed. It was a weird time.

In spite of changes and overall decrease in volume, the ER still had its busy days. Those days were fairly overwhelming. We would have a number COVID patients coming in; as all those who care for these patients knows, it's a very challenging and taxing series of hazmat changes, which are required anytime you enter the room of a COVID patient or suspected COVID patient. In addition, the use of an N95 mask makes it difficult to breathe. I noticed it most after walking around the ER with an N95, then trying to gown up for the COVID room and trying to speak loud enough for a patient to hear me. I would often have to stop and take a deep breath midsentence and then continue. As has been fairly well-documented in the media, at the end of the day, you are left sweaty, tired, and your face hurts from wearing the mask all day.

In the uncertain times, I was concerned about contracting the virus or even worse, bringing it home to my family. I would take all precautions before leaving the ER for the day. I would take a couple of extra antiseptic wipes to wipe down my vehicle when I got home, then I would change my clothes in the garage and place them in the laundry before fully entering the house. This required, of course, notifying everyone I was home and would be streaking directly through the house and into the shower. Fortunately, we were able to keep everyone at home safe from illness.

I had a number of direct exposures to COVID after intubating a couple that had arrived, in addition to some ICU patients who had taken a turn for the worse. As time passed, I became less worried about contracting the virus myself, likely just a function of my significant invincibility mantra. I continued to talk all precautions for sure, but I certainly didn't walk around scared or unwilling to help out with any sick patients in need of intubation.

Outside of work, we adjusted to the new realities of lockdown, like everyone else. One of our favorite pastimes was going out for a glass of wine and a nice meal. Now that was not an option; we made our happy hours and snacks. Jan had always been a very good cook and was great at coming up with happy hour at home ideas. We would often sit out on the back porch and listen to music and partake of whatever delicacy she was able to throw together. Thankfully, the wine stores stayed open, so we were always able to purchase wine as needed. We would FaceTime with Shelby and share virtual happy hour.

It was also during this time that we started to exercise a bit more. Jan and I had decided that we would try to do a few things together. We had never really done much exercise together beyond the occasional outing to hike or play tennis. Because of my prior work schedule, working in both the urgent care and ER, I would often have to just exercise when I could, leaving Jan to do here own thing on her own time as well. Now that I was in the ER full-time, we had more time off together, so we started walking and running together here and there. We tried to stay committed, but it was difficult. It was hot during the late spring and early summer in southern New Mexico, so running outside was challenging if not done in the early morning hours.

Over the first couple of months in the ER, which coincided with the first few months of the pandemic. I noted that my questions about the pending directorship position I was promised were starting to be dismissed. I would ask directly about when my start date would be, and I would receive an answer such as, "Well, administration wants me to stay in the position for another month or more to make sure things are stabilized." It appeared reasonable, again, given a pandemic. Yet Jan and I would often wonder to each other why it would matter all that much. In fact, given volumes were down overall, it might be the perfect time for me to take over and learn the administrative position.

The dismissiveness continued for the next few months; however, I was encouraged by the regional medical director to start thinking as the director and work with the advance practice providers and other physicians in the group regarding any changes they might want to implement and the direction they wanted the ER to take. I did so with full effort. I took the APPs to dinner one evening and got their feedback.

Like all of us, they had been frustrated by many things in the past, and they hoped they might have more of a voice with me in the director's position. I queried my physician colleagues, and they too were able to share some insight and ideas for change. I felt I had a good handle on what everyone wanted and how to bring a feeling of stability to our department. I just needed to get the final nod to take over the department.

The month before my heart attack. I noticed significant change in the interactions with the regional director. There was no longer mention of my taking over. My queries as to my status were either ignored or dismissed citing being too busy at work or travelling or the like. I was growing concerned. Finally, one afternoon, I requested an update on my status, and I received a text from the regional medical director: "administration wants an outside candidate." I was overwhelmed with anger. How could they do this to me? They had promised me the position and went so far as to have me start considering feedback from my colleagues to implement when I took over. What happened?

Unbeknownst to the regional medical director, or perhaps lazily forgotten, the "administration" she had referred to was only a couple of months ago my employer. I had a relationship with them, so I felt comfortable calling them to ask what had happened to my candidacy. I contacted them and was told they had no idea about what was texted to me. They would look into it. They did and got back to me within twenty-four hours; there was nothing to report. The ER staffing company had simply wanted to go with another candidate. It was ultimately the ER staffing company's call.

I was crushed. I was embarrassed to tell Jan what happened. I felt like the ultimate idiot, taken advantage of and manipulated by some unprofessional wretches. This all unfolded in early June, and it was two weeks before my heart attack.

I tried to gather more information from the staffing company, and I was told it would require an in-person conversation, and they were unable to do that at the moment. I would continue to be a part of the full-time staff, but there would be a new director. It was all so bewildering. As it turns out, there would never be a sit-down discussion. I would never really learn why I wasn't given the position, at least not from the staffing company.

It was Father's Day weekend. I was looking forward to playing golf with my buddy Jeremiah and my brother Isaac. It was going to be a good weekend. My brother was bringing his son along for the first nine holes; that was all he could muster in terms of attention span, but it was always fun to have him around. My dad was going to make the trip over from El Paso. It would be a great weekend.

Saturday before Father's Day came, and before golf, I wanted to get in a quick run because I knew I would likely have a few beers on the course and wanted to have my exercise for the day out of the way. I started to run up our street. I noticed I was having heartburn. *Hmm, weird*, I thought, *That was the third day in a row I had heartburn while running.* I had been taking some Mylanta as needed, and it seemed to help.

I tried to push through, which is what I had been doing, and I was usually able to get past it and get in a decent run. Only a week ago, I had run a hilly 2.5-mile track around the golf course and had run it in a reasonable time, and I felt great after. This time, though, I couldn't get it done. *To heck with it*, I thought. *I don't have it in me today to fight through. I'll just try to walk more while I golf.*

We set out to play golf. It was a beautiful hot sunny day with deep blue skies above; no wind. True to form, my nephew Ethan was joining us and in full energy form. Isaac was riding in a cart with our dad; I was riding with Jeremiah. It was always a good time with this crew. On the first two to three holes, I noticed some intermittent nausea; in fact, after putting out on the second hole, I was walking back to the cart and thought I might be sick. Isaac noticed, I was moving very slowly and asked, "Are you all right, bro?"

"Yeah, man, I'm good. Tummy is upset. I'm sure I'll be fine."

After a few minutes and making par on the next hole, I was fine. We enjoyed the day; we all had a few beers and then decided to move the celebration to my house. Jan's sister was in town visiting, along with her family. So they, along with my in-laws, met at my house to continue the early Father's Day celebration. I jumped in the pool when I got home; it had been hot out, and I was ready to cool off. As expected, the family showed up, and we all had a good time together. It was a nice early Father's Day celebration together. We were all weary of COVID, but we had all felt well, and those concerned wore their masks. There was no judgement; we wanted everyone to be comfortable.

The evening passed without incident. I was to bed early. I woke up early the next morning and noticed the heartburn was back. Damn, probably the result of multiple beers last night. I found the Mylanta and some tums. I tried to go back to bed to rest. I was up again a couple of hours later after hours of tossing and turning and trying to sleep more upright. The heartburn persisted. *That's weird*, I thought. *Usually, the burning goes away fairly quickly with medication.*

I got up to find some baking soda, an old-fashioned treatment, but couldn't seem to find it. I woke Jan to ask her; she helped me. I took a shot of baking soda water—gross, but I was desperate at this point. Jan went back to bed; I sat up in the living room. The pain worsened slightly and my concern started to grow. "Could this be something else?" I wondered. *I could easily run up to the ER and get my coworkers to run an EKG, just to be sure*, I thought. "No, don't be ridiculous. You always get annoyed when people go to the ER 'just to be sure,'" I reasoned.

I waited a bit longer and no improvement. I started to feel sick to my stomach and vomited. "I need to go in," I told myself. I started the shower to get cleaned up and dressed. Jan, startled by my vomiting, asked if I was okay. "I'm going to run up to the ER to be sure this isn't cardiac. I need an EKG," I told her matter-of-factly. I didn't want to be too dramatic or scare her.

"Babe, are you sure you're okay? I'm worried," she shared.

"Yes, I'm fine. I just need to be sure, and maybe they can give me some medicine to take care of the heartburn. I probably just need a GI cocktail!" I said by way of trying to address her concern.

As soon as I got out of the shower, I dressed quickly in a t shirt and shorts. I was feeling worse. The intensity of the pain was starting to be overwhelming. "Babe, I think I may need you to drive me up there," I confessed.

"Are you serious?" She immediately hopped out of bed. "I'm getting dressed right now!" She said in a stressed tone.

"Okay, I'm going to lay on the couch in the living room until you're ready," I said. The severity and intensity of the pain worsened. For so many years, I have heard patients describe their chest pain. It was always a large pressure-like sensation, like an elephant sitting on their chest, or a sharp, stabbing pain radiating to the neck and left arm. I couldn't quite articulate my pain in that same way. It felt like worsening heartburn but deep and nauseating.

Finally, I couldn't stand it anymore. "Babe, I think I need you to call an ambulance," I said, lying on the couch, growing more frightened. *God, could this really be a heart attack?*

Jan immediately dialed 911. "Yes, I think my husband is having a heart attack," Jan urgently said into the phone.

CHAPTER 3

ICU DELIRIUM

One of the most enduring feelings of the hospitalization was the feeling of anxiety and of uneasiness. If I felt pain in my chest, I imagined it would progress and kill me. If I felt sick to my stomach, I would vomit, and the thoughts would start racing: was I going to be able to stop, or would I continue and get dehydrated and have electrolyte imbalance, lose energy and pass out, or have a lethal arrhythmia and die? Everything that happened only triggered that feeling again. However, the worst part of all were the delusions and the delirium brought on by medications and a prolonged time spent in the ICU.

After awakening from the sedated state, I could not sleep. However, when I did close my eyes for an extended period, I had what became a recurring or ongoing nightmare, a nightmare so scary that it made me fear for my life and those that I loved. The nightmare wrapped itself in some component of reality, as in the nightmare I was sick in the ICU. The scary part was the gang of guys who were set about to hurt me and every member of my immediate family in order to extort money. The nightmare became so real, the fear so strong that I began requesting to be released from the hospital against medical advice. I never shared with any of the staff why I wanted to leave so desperately because I was unsure of who was working against me, but I had a strong sense if I could get out and get to my family, maybe we could drive to a big city and get away and hide, and I could find medical help there.

The nightmare would encompass my every night in the hospital. Every evening, as the sun began to set, after another dinner I didn't eat would be taken away, and I would prepare to try to sleep. I would start to fade and shortly the delusions would begin. The earliest thoughts of this delusion that I can remember began with the leader of this group, somehow coming by my room and threatening me and my family. He arrived under the guise that he was a close friend and just wanted to say hi; some of his friends worked in the hospital, so he was allowed in.

He stated specific means by which I was to make cash payments. Essentially, he was talking about having access to a credit card that I would need to pay for and also specific sports bets I would need to make each week. He liked golf, the NBA, and horse racing. He felt I needed to start paying him for having been so fortunate in my life, for doing well and living well, for practicing medicine, and for being, as he saw it, part of the wealthy few who needed to give back.

He was sure he deserved these reparations. He spoke of the cruel and violent manner in which he would hurt every member of my immediate family until I made the arrangements to deliver the money. In my delusion, it was clear he had access to the security and information technology departments in the hospital. Security would make sure he was always allowed in; they would station themselves near my room while he was in. They would flag him when someone else was entering the room. The information tech guys made it so that he could call into my room without being found out. He got access to my computer and my life, so he knew where I would be when I got out. He demanded money that I didn't have. After multiple failed attempts to convince him that I didn't have the kind of money he was wanting, he somehow sent me videos of my family being attacked and injured by his hired hands. I was devastated that my family was under attack while I was sick and in the hospital.

In reality, I was alone in my room, the nurse stationed outside my door, but I was frightened beyond measure. I had to get out of the hospital. I asked my nurse multiple times that I be allowed to sign out against medical advice. A colleague of mine, who was a charge nurse in the emergency room, was called over one night when I persisted in asking to be allowed to leave AMA. He was a very kind and mild-mannered person. He was well respected in the hospital, so he answered the call, and he came in to see me, and he tried to talk me down. It was interesting because I had the thought that the ER was not connected to the ICU I was in. I'm not sure why, but I was under the impression he had to drive over to see me, and in fact, I think I mentioned something to him about how nice it was of him to take the time to do so. The reality is that the ER and ICU are separated by locked double doors. I had been through those doors many times in the past to answer an emergency call or code blue within the ICU.

In my mind, I wasn't completely sure he was on my side. I wasn't exactly sure who was on my side. While the leader of the malicious group had visited, I noticed that he had said hi to a few people who walked around outside my room, so I felt he had a constant connection or lookout around. I tried to think it through; how could I get out? I was in no shape to run or even move quickly. I still needed medication. How could I make it? And so it would go each night.

As the delirium persisted, the delusions would begin each evening. If I didn't hear from the group's leader, which was less often toward the end of my hospitalization, then the visions would start with people coming in my room and setting up a party. Somehow, they were able to hide themselves from nurses and others that came in my room. They carried large invisibility cloaks or screens that they hid behind when people walked in. They played loud music and began to party in my room and proceed to taunt me and kept me from resting. They would turn up the sound on the TV to try and cover up the sounds of people partying. They disconnected the nurse call button so I wouldn't call the nurse in for help. I surmised they were trying to not only scare me but mentally fatigue me so that I would agree to their demands. How could I heal if I couldn't rest? How would I get rid of them before I was discharged home?

Ultimately, the delusions lightened to some degree. I don't remember seeing anyone in my room the last night or two. In reality, I was unsure if the bad characters were just waiting for me to be released or if they were truly gone. It was hard to know what was real. One night, after being moved to a regular hospital room from the

ICU and about two to three days before I was discharged, I woke up from a very brief sleep to find flooded floors as a result of water leaking from behind my hospital bed. I called for the nurse. She walked in; I noticed she never struck water. I was aware enough of my confusion to know I might be imagining it all. I asked her to confirm she saw no water on the floor. She pleasantly and sweetly said, "No, I don't see water. Maybe you just had a bad dream." I could not escape it. It was frightening.

When I was moved to a regular non-ICU medical floor, we believed I might be able to rest better. However, I continued to not sleep for longer than a half hour. It was such an issue that as the nurses changed shifts and signed out to one another, I overheard them report, "Check on him at night because he doesn't sleep." The nurses were always so good to me, whether they took extra good care of me because I was a physician or because they believed I might call them out on some perceived mistreatment is hard to know. But I had little concern that they would and could take good care of me as my thoughts were overwhelmed by the delusions and the growing anxiety that encompassed me each night.

As the time for me to be discharged from the hospital neared, I was becoming more and more anxious. I couldn't go long without Jan at my side. The nights seemed to be getting longer. Soon, my hospital doctor indicated I was getting close to discharge, but they wanted to be sure to do it on a weekday when all ancillary services were available. I couldn't wait!

Finally, the day to be discharged came. I, of course, didn't sleep again the night prior. I was fully awake and ready for each doctor's visit by 5:00 a.m. I awaited the various specialist and finally the all-controlling hospitalist. He was a colleague of mine, but in this scenario, he held my life in his hands, and I feared he might find good reason I shouldn't be discharged. Were my discharge day labs not normal? Was there a complication with being discharged home in the middle of a pandemic? Would my wife be allowed to come pick me up? Did the physical therapist feel I couldn't go home? I tried to think of every potential disruption to my plan to go home and tried to make my brain work to be certain I could counter any possible argument they might make to keep me in this place, where delusions, delirium, and anxiety reigned.

"Of course you're going home today. Everything looks great!" said the wonderful hospitalist, who may have sensed some urgency in my question. "I just need to get with your cardiologist to make sure your special device is ready to go home with you and make sure PT/OT have all signed off on outpatient therapy. The discharge planner will stop by to coordinate all of that."

I knew this routine, but it was reassuring to hear it all from him. As predicted, they all came by; however, there was a sudden potentially large complication. The discharge planner arrived to discuss the details of my discharge "Okay, Dr. Acosta, where would you like to do your inpatient rehab?" she asked. *Inpatient rehab?* I was immediately sucked into the anxiety that *I wasn't* getting out of the hospital! They found a way to keep me. It had to have something to do with the bad guys from my delusion! How could they control my life so dramatically?

The fear blasted in; I couldn't do it! "I don't want inpatient therapy!" I practically screamed. "I'm fine. I can walk. I have a family at home if I need anything!"

The discharge planner thankfully conceded that maybe that was possible, but she would need to check it out! My fear continued until which time she kindly returned to say outpatient therapy was fine. I did it!

As anyone who has ever been in a hospital might understand, getting discharged is a process, and none of the processes go fast and certainly are never completed in a reasonable amount of time. The first indication the discharge was going to take a while was with the arrival of the special equipment salesman. He was a very kind and loquacious gentlemen who brought in my "life vest." A life vest is a wearable external cardiac defibrillator, something I was told by my cardiologist, would likely be necessary to provide us all some peace of mind after I was discharged. There was a period of time after a patient suffers a heart attack that the patient is susceptible to sudden death due to a lethal arrhythmia. The life vest was designed to sense such an event and deliver a lifesaving jolt of electricity to get the heart back in a normal sinus rhythm, thereby saving your life.

The duration of my time with the vest was not clearly established, but I was absolutely willing, as long as it meant I could go home. The vest was built like a women's bra without the breast cups. The device clasped in the front, midchest, and held sensors and electrical pads over the heart and back, ready to deliver a shock if an abnormal heart rhythm was sensed. This contraption then plugged into a large battery pack that was carried by a strap over your shoulder, like those portable oxygen machines you see people with emphysema use. The technician went to remarkable lengths to be sure my wife, and I understood all the instructions. With each word and sentence, he was prolonging my stay in the hospital. Finally, after sensing my obvious disinterest and growing frustration, he simply said, "My card is here. Please call me if you have any questions," and he was gone!

That meant I was done! I was ready to go! I called the nurse to notify here I was ready to sign discharge paperwork. "I'm sorry, Dr. Acosta. I haven't seen the home oxygen folks, and I need to have that delivered before you go. Also, I need to run a COVID test before you leave," she informed me sheepishly, sensing my growing anger.

"Please do the COVID swab now, but I'm not waiting for oxygen, and I'm not waiting for the COVID results if you're not going to run a rapid test. I will just sign out against medical advice," I said, trying to calm the anger growing in me. I knew this was just protocol, and they didn't really think I had COVID. *Stay calm*, I told myself. *You're just going to hurt yourself, and at worst, you may make them believe you're not fit for discharge.*

After more time passed—and well after lunchtime, which I had set as my latest departure time—my kind nurse returned and indicated she had gotten special permission to allow me to leave. "I'll get the forms to sign, and you're out of here!"

Of course, she didn't return in a time I felt was reasonable, so I began the discharge myself. "Babe, hand me that gauze over on that counter and grab that Coban roll," I directed my wife. "Do you think you can pull this IV out?" I asked. She wasn't medical, but she was a mom; nothing could scare her, I thought.

"No, just wait for the nurse, I don't want to mess anything up," she said in her stern but kind voice.

"Oh, c'mon, I've done this plenty of times. I'll walk you through it," I said as I pulled the tape loose from around the IV in my arm. She realized it was coming out regardless, so she kindly pulled when I said pull! I placed the gauze over the IV site and held pressure for what seemed like minutes. I peeked under the gauze after some time. *Still significant venous ooze*, I thought. *Hmm, damn. I forgot I'm on blood thinners now. I'm a bleeder—another life changer.*

I continued to hold pressure until my fingers started to tire. "Babe, would you grab more gauze and hold it tight on there for a minute?" I asked my wife. She obliged, and we were able to get it to slow, and then she wrapped some Coban around it per my instructions.

We sat there waiting. "You know what, babe, just go get the car. I'm walking out!" I said, finally fed up with the discharge process.

"No, just be patient. She's going as fast as she can," Jan tried to calm me.

"I know she is, but I'm not the only patient up here, and I know it'll be another hour at least for the oxygen people to get here," I pleaded.

Jan, growing uncomfortable with my efforts, walked out and found a nurse. "He's walking out. Can you please just discharge us?" she pleaded.

I was mentally preparing myself to just walk out. Typically and ceremonially, patients are carted out in a wheelchair to help the newly healed manage the long distance out of a hospital comfortably to a waiting vehicle outside but also so patients don't fall and harm themselves on the way out. I wasn't sure I could get to the elevator and out the front door without hurting myself, but the fear and anxiety of having to wait any longer was great motivation to try.

Finally, the nurse arrived; as I had anticipated, she had been called to help with another patient, and the oxygen people still hadn't shown up. But again, she said she was allowed to let me sign the discharge papers and get wheeled out now. "But first, let me wipe off all that blood on your arm and get a new bandage for the old IV site.

You pulled it out yourself, huh?" the nurse stated by way of making a dig at the mess I had made.

Off ran Jan to get the car, and I hopped in the wheelchair, ready to smell the outdoor air. It was sunny and hot out. I saw Jan in the car; she parked right out the front door. I encouraged my wheelchair driver to stop and let me walk from the hospital front door. I walked fast, steadily, and directly to our vehicle, Jan opening the door for me; nothing was going to keep me from going home today. I didn't turn to wave. No goodbyes; let's just get the hell out of here.

CHAPTER 4

GOING HOME

Driving up the street to our home was exciting. I was so ecstatic to be outside the hospital. I was now riding down the streets; only days before, I could only stare outside my window and imagine what it would be like to actually be heading this direction again. While I was overwhelmingly happy to be going home, it occurred to me that I had missed lunch due to the prolonged discharge. As it turns out, when you're a patient in the hospital, if you don't order your lunch by midmorning, you are not on the list to receive a tray. Given I was being discharged, I didn't bother with the lunch order, especially since I desired to leave that place well before noon. As we drove and got closer to home, I was not feeling great. I began to feel the severe hunger pains, light-headedness, and weakness associated with missing a meal. The symptoms seemed more intense since I didn't have much in terms of reserves after what I had been through.

As we pulled into our driveway, I witnessed one of the most truly special and touching sights in my life. Our kids were standing outside with welcome home signs! They had big homemade signs and had welcome home music playing. It was the *Rocky* theme! I fought back the tears. Today was a happy day! I popped open the door. I was feeling dizzy and tired. I quickly thanked the kids and told them I needed to get inside and get a snack and rest. A bit of a buzzkill, but I felt I had to be honest. I could no longer trust myself with any symptoms and could not assume all would be fine.

I managed to get inside and get some simple sugars and fell into my chair. Within fifteen minutes, I was feeling better; the kids gathered around, and one by one, we shared our first hugs since the day I died. Home felt every bit as good as I had imagined. The scent of the air, the comfort of the furniture, the inside temperature were all perfect. All punctuated, of course, by the welcome home licks of our German shepherd Delilah! However, in the back of my mind, the concern about my delusions being true remained. How would I tell my wife about them now that I was home? Would she think me not well and try to go back to the hospital? Things to worry about another day. I was home with my family all together. We were so close to it never happening. Thank God.

Together, we all got used to me being home but still very early in recovery mode. Everyone ran around making sure I had everything I needed: a glass of water, a healthy snack, a soft pillow to nap on, a blanket in case the air conditioning was too much. The family truly came together; it was endearing. I was so proud of our kids, for they stepped up in the time of need and filled a role left empty by my illness.

It was only after being home that I realized the magnitude of what had happened and how it had affected so many. I started to receive texts from well-wishers, many friends, and colleagues; even former bosses reached out. My little brother Isaac would text to check on me and would have my nephew Ethan send videos to lift my spirits. It made me feel better too, knowing I wasn't at it alone. There were so many grand gestures; it's hard to recount them all. Jan and the kids all made me giant get well cards. Since these could not be taken to the hospital and posted in my room, they saved them all for me. They were all very sweet, emotional words written by our three kids. Friends started sending meals and letters of encouragement. The girls would cook and let Jan and me rest together on the couch, just enjoying the moments of being alive.

I would be moved by each and every letter. Friends and family were so articulate in their cards and letters, each recounting their sincere thoughts and concerns about me and how unbelievable the events that unfolded were. Two of my former bosses, CEOs of the hospitals, reached out and let me know they had been and were praying for me. My mother-in-law and sisters-in-law sent amazing prayers. They had prayed for me via text while I was in the hospital, and Jan would them read aloud—amazing women all. The many texted prayers and words of encouragement were great sources of strength. I felt important to many and thus felt the strength to get well.

One of my very best friends from medical school took the time to send a typewritten letter. His words were sobering; the news of my near demise had shaken him. He shared that he had openly wept upon hearing the news. This event had taken a toll on us all. As he typed so well, we should all dedicate ourselves to living life.

Each day, Jan continued to share with me what life was like while I was in the hospital. Our oldest daughter, Shelby, had flown in the day of the event after being called by Jan. She was allowed to see me very briefly in the ICU after getting into town from the airport. Jan brought her up to the hospital to potentially say their very last words to me. It was hard to hear the recounting of their day and the days that followed as they sat and prayed and waited, not knowing if I would survive.

Jan and Shelby, consistent with their nature, set up a form of communications network while I was in the ICU. Jan would take a group of people and contact all of them via text with updates for each day and then individually answer any questions they had. Shelby would take a different group and keep them updated each day and answer any of their questions. Together, they would group text or call our "medical" friends and gather thoughts and potential questions for the doctors. Our niece Amanda, an internal medicine resident in Fort Worth, would gather information and share with Shelby and Jan. As Jan relayed, these group calls ultimately became the most entertaining sessions of the day, as my friends are, to say the least, confident and each with their own expertise had many thoughts to share. Ultimately, they all had a sense with each update that things were not going well those initial two to three days. My friend Joe, never one to mince words would simply share, "Well, that doesn't sound good to me."

Jan, Shelby, Luke, and Anna would then prepare for the daily FaceTime encounters with the cardiologist and then later, each of the kind ICU nurses who were so sweet to take the time to provide updates each shift. Jan shared that my brother Isaac would leave his job during his lunch hour in order to be present for the midday FaceTime update from the doctors. It easily brings me to tears to think of how much this kindness meant to our family, for the kids to see me hanging on, to know that I was still here. Nonetheless, because circumstance dictated, they all filled a role, whether it was mowing the lawn, taking care of the cars, cleaning house, cooking meals.

As I would have guessed, some of our very best friends drove to town immediately upon hearing the news from Jan. Pandemic be damned. They came and stayed in town, stayed close to Jan and the kids and helped in whatever capacity was needed, performing all the unspoken kindnesses: cleaning up, washing dishes, buying groceries and paper goods—whatever it took to help. I was told that at one point, on the day I arrived in the emergency room, the hospital personnel allowed all of my visitors in one waiting room, secluded from everyone else. They had all arrived and sat there in support of me. They all came to be a comfort to Jan, Shelby and Luke, and Annalise and my brother Isaac.

They all sat their together and heard the overhead calls for "code blue" and then waited anxiously as the charge nurse would come in and inform them, "His heart stopped again, but we got him back," or the dreaded solemn face that would come out and inform them, "His heart has stopped. We are doing all we can, but things are not looking good." Jan told me of the specific time in the day she was asked if she wanted to come in and watch. As she told me the story, it struck me; this was something we did in the ER when our efforts were starting to look futile. We would invite family members in so they could see for themselves the great lengths the ER team was going through to save their loved one. It allowed them to see the large group of people invested specifically in saving a life. To see the many nurses and techs taking turns performing CPR. To see the respiratory team breathing each breath for their loved one. To see the anguish and determination on the face of the doctor thinking through each moment to be sure no possibility went unconsidered.

After hearing the stories, I was immediately sad for Jan that she had to hear those words, that she had to walk down that hall and stand in that room alone watching the team work on me. It was too much for anyone. She ultimately excused herself from the trauma bay, in which I was being resuscitated, and waited outside in the waiting room with the others.

I was glad to be home, but I was so sad to know what my family had been through. As each day at home would turn into night, I started to develop a sense of dread. I was growing tired and sleepy, but I continued sleeping very little. It seemed to worsen each night: awake every hour or two, get out of bed for a minute to walk around, each time out of bed taking maximum effort to gather the wires of my life vest and of course, the damn battery pack. I tried some OTC meds for sleep, which didn't seem to help. I would get up at 2:00 or 3:00 a.m., walk to the kitchen, stare out the large bay window. With a view across the valley, I could see the airport at the west end of town, where I used to fly. I thought of the number of times I went out to practice flying in the pattern and lowering that Piper Cherokee for a touch and go and finally to a full stop. It had been a fun endeavor. The memories actually stirred up anxiety in me, thinking of how dangerous that was. How did I do that only months ago?

I imagined who else might be awake and working. I thought of my colleagues working in the ER and how busy they might be. I wondered if I'd ever be strong enough to do that again, but I was in no hurry to find out. I'd sit in my chair in the living room and stare at the TV with the power off. I didn't want to wake anyone, given it was a nightly occurrence. I would find out later, each night my wife lay in bed, listening and trying to sleep with one eye open, so to speak, making sure I was okay. Shelby, our eldest, would sleep in the media room just off the main living room; she later told us she would hear me milling around and listen and occasionally peek in on me to be sure I was okay. It was hard for all of us.

I tried to use my clinical skill and knowledge to figure out why I couldn't sleep. I thought of everything, and I feared that it might be anxiety. I was afraid of that diagnosis. I could think of nothing scarier than having no control over your thoughts and fears and the idea that it could spiral uncontrollably was overwhelming.

As the morning sun rose, I would welcome another day, sleepy but very happy to be alive. I started an exercise regimen, walking on the sidewalk in front of my house. There was a considerable incline from west to east; it was challenging. I would be starting cardiac rehab in a week, and I wanted to be ahead of the curve. I also had physical therapy, occupational therapy, and speech and language therapy evaluations coming up. I wanted to shine when the time arrived. So I walked out front at first five to six passes on the sidewalk, the width of the front yard, then I increased to eight to ten passes. I felt good walking. I felt close to being me, yet I had a significant and quick onset of fatigue. I was definitely deconditioned, I thought, or was this my new life with heart failure following a heart attack? God, I hoped not.

I figured with increased exercise I might rest better at night—no such luck. And so it went for a week longer: slow physical gains, constant fatigue, no sleep. One afternoon, my wife and I were on our way to get a Sonic drink, a new daily ritual we started in order to get out of the house and have something to look forward to. She told me that our youngest, Anna, was going to a social event with a friend. There were very limited events during the pandemic.

Panic set in, I didn't want her to go. I still feared the bad actors from the delusions that threatened to hurt me and my family were still out and waiting for their time to come and collect. I had to tell Jan before something happened. I mustered up the strength to tell her all about what it was that I was afraid of and of what I had dreamed or imagined or actually experienced. It was all still so hard to tell what had been real and what wasn't.

She could tell immediately something was very wrong; it wasn't the most common thing for me to say I was afraid or incapable. She reached out for my arm while she was driving us to Sonic and said, "All of that was just a dream. We are all safe. The kids are fine, and you're safe." I didn't realize how much that was weighing on me. I felt a sudden relief and realized I had been building up such a large vat of fear and anxiety for a multitude of reasons associated with my hospitalization. It was right then and there that I decided I needed some help.

I called my PCP, who, as it turns out, was one of my students while she was training. She very kindly and patiently listened to my troubles and agreed we needed to act on this quickly. She provided me a prescription that would help me rest and also treat the anxiety at night. I was worried about taking this medication. I had prescribed it hundreds of times over the years, for the very same indication, always after careful consideration. I was afraid it might not work, or worse yet, work so well that it became addicting. However, I was not doing well, and I needed help—all very tough to admit. So I tried it. it worked better than I could have asked. I slept fully and deeply and without bad dreams or delusions! Consequently, I woke up feeling better and rested. It only took a couple of nights of using it to reset my sleeping pattern; the anxiety calmed. I was able to stop it, after just those few days. It gave me hope of brighter days, my first breakthrough on the comeback.

CHAPTER 5

REHAB

I had lost quite a bit of weight during my hospitalization, but even more came off after being home. With a very strict cardiac diet in place and a limited appetite, I got very thin and looked the part of my childhood nickname Flaco. I could see it in the eyes of my brother and parents when they each visited after I got home. It was good to see everyone. They all had comments on how skinny I was; it wasn't glowing praise.

I had gained some weight over the last couple of years, in spite of exercising; with the long work hours and poor diet, I was adding a few pounds each year. With so few days off due to my own hard-headed desire to make more money, I would make the most of those days off: a quick run, clearly not long enough or frequent enough to maintain weight or conditioning; golf with my buddy Jeremiah or with my brother Ike (on really good days, it would be both of them); a few cold beers, possibly a happy hour snack after, where Jan would join us, then wine and dinner. It was a typical day off routine.

Now, I would vow to keep that under better control, but being so thin, I felt small and weak and had difficulty with temperature regulation, I had to wear extra clothing to stay warm inside the house. It was July in Las Cruces, the temperature outside consistently one hundred degrees Fahrenheit, yet I would often sit inside under a blanket and would have to occasionally take a walk outside to warm up.

The time for initiating cardiac rehab and going through all my therapeutic assessments had arrived. Jan dutifully drove me to my appointments. We arrived one sunny, hot afternoon at the physical and occupational therapy center. It was odd being the patient. I knew the processes behind the counter and in the exam rooms, but I now had to sit and wait patiently to be called up, be asked all the typical biographical information, the so-called demographics. I would often be recognized by personnel and be told of thoughts and prayers that had been sent on my behalf. In fact, one afternoon, weeks later, while getting a follow-up outpatient X-ray, I was checking in for the study, and a passerby overheard my name and stopped and called out to me, "Hi, Dr. Acosta. I'm so happy to see you are doing well."

People were always so kind. "Thank you so much. I really appreciate that," I said, not knowing who she was.

After I completed my X-ray, the young lady at the check-in desk stopped me on my way out and said, "Here you go. Someone left this for you." She handed me a folded note. In it, a lady had written.

> I wanted you to know that we heard about your recent health issues from our daughter, who works here in the hospital with you. We put you on our prayer list and each of our family prayed to God every day that you would be healed. It is such a blessing to see you doing so well. God Bless.

I was astounded at the kindness. I smiled.

So after a short wait in the waiting room, I was called in for the PT evaluation; it was patients only allowed. Interactions with therapists or technicians were often a little bit odd at first, being a physician. Everyone assumes you know everything that happens in all forms of medical and therapy clinics, which couldn't be further from the truth. The PT explained she would perform her assessment, then she would let the OT know I was ready for that assessment immediately after we were done. The PT started: typical range of motion movements, then strength testing in all extremities, standing, bending, balance. "All good, Doc. You're fine. No need for therapy."

I was happy, albeit a little surprised. I was feeling stronger and certainly could perform each of the tasks asked without difficulty. The OT evaluation followed, this time smaller movements, more manual dexterity type assessments. Same conclusion: no need for therapy. *Shoot, maybe I survived and got better!* I laughed at that thought.

A few days later, it would be the speech language assessment. Again, a very kind and proficient therapist called me in. Jan was allowed to go in with me for this one. There was nothing taken for granted here; the therapist was well aware most physicians likely didn't know the extent of the assessments performed by speech-language therapists beyond knowing to order her assessments after a patient suffered a stroke. She explained she would assess my speech, understanding, and memory.

My memory! I hadn't thought of that! Had my mind been affected by the heart attack? Had I forgotten any critical or necessary knowledge? I had always taken pride in having good memorization and recall skills. It was the basis for my success in school. I hadn't felt that I had any deficiency, but then I hadn't really been challenged in any way other than to state my name, the date, and my location. It was an interesting visit. I read, recognized, recalled, and repeated. It was challenging and fatiguing, but I felt like all was going well.

One of the final components was repeating a story after it had been read in full to me. I managed to get most of the details on that one. Finally, I repeated a long string of numbers after they were read aloud to me. It seemed like strings of twelve to fifteen numbers. I'm sure it wasn't quite that many. Nonetheless, I did it! "Dr. Acosta, it was an honor having you in our clinic today. You did great!"

Certainly, there was some degree of hyperbole in the statement, but the very kind therapist made her point. My memory was fine, no need for speech and language therapy—another mark to check off the list and an important one. Interestingly, as she reviewed my performance in each section, she noted that I scored lowest on the component of the test where I was supposed to list all the vegetables I could think of in one minute. Certainly, there needed to be some changes in my life.

Jan dropped me off at cardiac rehab later in the week. I had been making my walks daily in front the house, even stretching my distance to include a portion of the neighbor's front yards. I knew I was ready for rehab. The cardiac rehab nurse was no-nonsense but kind. She knew who I was. She was a veteran nurse; she wasn't going to let me get away with anything. It felt great to work out and stretch, but I was hesitant to push myself too hard. I had a cardiac monitor on, so I took comfort in knowing if things got too crazy, an alarm might let me know. Also, I still had the damn life vest on, so if needed, I would get a big shock!

I shared with the cardiac rehab nurse that I wasn't excited about wearing the vest. She proceeded to tell me her story with regard to the vest. Her husband had an MI some years back and was supposed to also get and wear a vest, but he decided not to. One day out, while he was out at the golf course, he suffered that dreaded cardiac rhythm complication and died. She had properly scared me into compliance.

The bigger point of concern may have been that I was the youngest patient in the room by at least twenty years, possibly thirty. I had to outdo these old guys! I went about each exercise determined to maximize the gain. I completed the approximately forty-five-minute treatment. I felt very good. Jan had been anxious to hear how it went for me; she was waiting patiently outside. The truth be told, she was not yet ready to leave me all alone there, so she never really left the rehab building; she did her own workout outside the building during the time I was inside. I happily reported that I had done everything asked of me and felt I could have done more.

In the weeks that came, I would dutifully show up for rehab, three times a week, and Jan or Shelby would pick me up. I was making gains. I was crushing all the old guys! I even used the heaviest weights they had for the strength exercises—no mercy. On off-days, Jan and I or Jan and Shelby and I would exercise on our own, walking around the neighborhood or at the public exercise area at New Mexico State University. Soon, it was time for my next cardiology follow-up appointment. I was excited because at my previous and initial outpatient visit, Dr. Ponce indicated I could potentially get rid of my life vest. It was so uncomfortable and such a nuisance to carry around; I would be glad to get rid of it at the first chance!

Fortunately, I never had a serious alarm on it, although, one afternoon, I got up out of my chair and walked out back near the pool just to feel the sun and stretch my legs. Suddenly the mechanical voice of the life vest came on, "Abnormal rhythm detected. Please press the button," or something similar. *Oh shit!* I thought. I moved quickly to get in the house in case I passed out or got shocked or whatever was supposed to happen next. I quickly found the response button on the battery pack unit. Then nothing; it went back in its silent monitoring mode. *Whew!* I thought, *I'll be damn glad to get rid of this thing.*

And so the day of the clinic visit with the cardiologist arrived, and Jan and I, in our new capacity as patient and wife, waited patiently in the waiting room to be called back. Once we were called back and placed in a room, the doctor arrived, and we worked through progress in rehab, symptoms, medication tolerance. We discussed the feelings of fatigue, possibly due to beta blockers. "Maybe we can take those at night," she offered. A persistent dry cough, "Maybe it was the ace inhibitor. Let's switch to an ARB," she directed.

I quickly asked about the vest. "Oh, yes," said Dr. Ponce. "Your EF has improved. It's not quite normal but good enough, and also, you're outside the window that we see sudden cardiac death post MI."

"Great news!" I said. I took my shirt off right then and removed the life vest. Thanks for being there, Mr. Vest, but good riddance.

"Okay, we'll see you in a month or so for a repeat echo, and maybe we can get rid of blood thinners!" she offered.

"I can't wait for that!" I said, another small victory!

A week or so later, another day I had been waiting for arrived—the day to once again jog. I had built it up in my mind. I was going to be a runner again, a poor runner but a runner nonetheless; it felt a million miles away from where I was at that point when I first started rehab. I was concerned that it might be too much, that I might develop chest pain or shortness of breath to the degree, that I couldn't recover and pass out. In short, it was a major milestone in my mind.

The rehab nurse nonchalantly said, "Are you ready?" I said yes, and we turned up the rate on the treadmill, and off I went. No problem; I ran three minutes. Wow! I couldn't wait to tell Jan when I was done. It felt great to share good news with everyone. I texted our good friends, my brother. Once I started, the floodgates were open, I felt good jogging lightly. I worked to exceed all the timed running rotations at cardiac rehab. Jan and I started jogging during our off-day walks. Then it occurred to us. We should run a 5K! We talked about it and wondered aloud if we could do it! Jan, as determined as ever and admittedly never much for running, was in; we would do our first 5K together.

We searched and found a 5K in Dallas, where Shelby lived; we would do the Turkey Trot on Thanksgiving and then celebrate as a family. Along the way of my improvement, it came time for Shelby to return to her home in Dallas. It was clear I was doing well in my recovery, and she had a life she had put on hold in order to be with us. It was the most extended time we had spent together since she graduated from college. She always visited during holidays and might stay a week or two, but she always was off living her life. It was also the most time our blended family had ever spent together! It was awesome to have her home. First, because I felt most comfortable with all the kids at home. With the ongoing COVID pandemic and the unsettling events that landed me in the hospital, I needed everyone close to know we were all okay. Second, she was a full adult now. She helped make decisions; she helped to care for me; she helped around the house. I wanted her to stay, but I knew she needed to go. And so, with tears flowing, we helped her pack her car and watched as she drove off. I had written her a note and placed it in her car to read later. I was proud of her.

As I continued to improve and our running proficiency gained steam, the thoughts of potentially returning to work started to creep in. I contacted my employer. We made initial plans for me to return. I would start at the "small" ER with half shifts. We used the term "small" ER to describe a freestanding ER associated with the hospital, with the main ER being located in the typical location prominently positioned on the first floor of the main building of the hospital. I was feeling like I might make it all the way back, although I continued to get significantly fatigued. I was napping most days after lunch. I told my myself I would be fine, and I was going to do it. I started reading medical literature again. I reviewed EKGs and X-rays online just to freshen my memory. I started reading books for leisure to get my mind back in shape. Jan had bought me crossword and mathematic puzzles to help sharpen all aspect of my brain. We were on the proper path.

I was excited to get back to work, to have some sense of normalcy. I wasn't quite the person I was before the MI, but I was feeling good. I had to have one more cardiology appointment and get the official release to work. I had done well without the life vest. An updated echo continued to show improvement, although again, we weren't quite normal. "You are okay to return to work. No problem. Things look great!" she shared.

I was excited but not surprised. "Um, Doctor, do you think it would be okay to have some wine now?" I was somewhat anxious to try a drink again just to feel normal.

"Yes, enjoy. Just don't overdo it." The final advice, of course—not so much clinical but more of a caretaker's concern.

Yes! She must really feel I am doing well! I thought to myself.

The day of my first shift back was exciting. Jan took pics of me, like the first day of school. It had been approximately sixty days since my MI. It seemed like forever but really wasn't that long ago. I had improved so much; I was starting to forget how weak I felt initially. Jan packed me extra snacks and drinks just in case.

I hadn't driven myself much in the time I was home because I frankly didn't need to. So simply driving to work was a major step. The first shift would only be four to six hours; they allowed me the flexibility for whatever I could tolerate. There would be another doctor working, so there was no pressure to carry the load, or I could simply duck out if it was too much. The staff couldn't have been nicer: hugs all around, congratulatory handshakes, good thoughts, people sharing their version of events during my hospitalization—

again, stories of prayers and of concerned staff members, briefly stopping by my room in the hospital to wish me well.

So the shift began. It felt good. Computer passwords, documentation, physical exam, lab orders—it all came flowing back. I was going to be okay. It turned out the doctor working that day had his own ideas about what my time working would mean for him. He disappeared for the remainder of the time I was there. I found out later, he mentioned to staff he wanted to see if I was really okay to return or not. His manner of doing so was to leave the workload to me for the duration of my shift, as though it was his decision. What a dope! Didn't he know I was restored? Little did I know how much his views would come into play later.

I couldn't wait to get home that evening and tell Jan how I did, like a schoolkid coming home with my first A on an assignment. We celebrated in small way at home that night. I had been on my feet for a more extended time than I had been in a while. I definitely got tired and consequently rested very well at night. I worked a couple of more partial shifts and gained more confidence with each passing shift. As it turns out, none of the remaining doctors I worked with felt the need to determine on their own if I was okay to work alone. They accepted me back as a colleague, and we shared the load. It was nice to feel a part of the team again.

Coincidentally, one of those partial shifts I worked was with a relatively new doctor to our ER staff. She flew in from Utah to help cover shifts. That day, I walked into the ER and recognized her name. I introduced myself. "Hi, I'm Steve. I'm working a partial shift today with you. I'm working my way back into fighting shape," I joked. "I think we've met before, but I wasn't quite myself."

"Oh my god, it is so nice to meet you!" she said.

Still in the time of COVID, it was hard to know if handshakes or fist bumps were most appropriate, so we kind of waived at each other. She was the physician on duty in the main ER, on Father's Day, the morning I came in and challenged her clinical skills. "Do you mind if I give you a hug to thank you?" I asked, not wanting to be too weird or too forward.

"Of course not," she replied.

"Thank you so much for saving me. My family and I really appreciate it. Well, I think my family does anyway!" I tried to joke so as not to make it too emotional an encounter since we were at work, after all.

I went about saying hi to the rest of the staff and logging in to the computer to get to work. From the small doctor's office, the doctor poked her head out and asked, "Would you think it weird if I asked to take a picture with you?"

"Of course not. I'd be honored," I said.

"It's not often you get to meet the people you save!" she said by way of explaining the request. It was new for all of us.

I worked a couple more half shifts without issue. I got and felt stronger with each passing day. I was ready for full shifts. I contacted the scheduler and let her know. She assured me she would schedule full shift but fewer than a typical full-time load; it would be best to ease back into the fray. I was excited. Slowly, I was getting to where I wanted to be.

CHAPTER 6

RECOVERY

Jan and I developed a good routine: wake up early relatively early; have some decaf, a healthy light breakfast; watch the *Today* show; and check the stock market (we were now full-time amateur stock option traders). Jan had taken over the finances during my hospitalization, which was a chore, while I had available a list of bills and the date they were due and all the payments made each month. There were some not on the list that I got e-mail reminders for; there were multiple banks. Jan had her work cut out for her. To her credit, she managed it all, even made some suggestions on how I might do it better.

We would sit together and go over everything, and we found ways to more efficiently share the burden of paying bills and keeping track of investments and savings. Since I was back working, we needed to figure out how much I was going to need to work in order for us to survive. Although I was yearning for normalcy, I didn't want to fall back into the typical routine of working and overworking myself. If I was going to learn any lesson from all of this, it would be that I needed to cut back in lots of ways. If we could do better controlling expenses, we wouldn't need to make so much money, and therefore, I could work less and spend more time maintaining a healthy lifestyle. We made it our plan. Maybe we could even manage things so well, we could cut back to working half time! Thankfully, we had done very well saving money, and now that I was working again, we had hope that we wouldn't have a full financial collapse.

We went out for dinner here and there. We had some wine. It felt like a new normal.

Somewhere along the way, a colleague and friend from my hometown hospital and my previous place of employment contacted me. They needed help covering a couple of ER shifts a few days before my birthday. I was excited to be asked and excited to make some money. Helping out in their ER was something I had done here and there whenever they needed an extra doctor. Typically, Dr. Carver, the ER director, would call, and I'd help if I could. I hadn't yet worked a full shift, but I thought I would have no problem. The hospital, per protocol, asked for all the proper documentation that I was indeed fully released to work, which I gladly, if not proudly, sent to them. Jan and I made plans to make the trip.

We texted our friends Jessica and Schylar to let them know we were headed to town in a couple weeks. We were not only excited to get out of town for the first time but also happy to be returning to my hometown to work and see our friends. Given it was close to my birthday, we thought we could see our friends and hang out, work, and then possibly take a short trip after to Lubbock, Texas, to see my medical school buddy. We were excited to see everyone and thank everyone in person for their support and excited to have this change in our routine.

We made the nearly four-hour drive to my hometown. We had made arrangements to see our friends early that afternoon the day before I was to work. Our closest friends there were sisters Sky and Jess; they were the best of people. Sky had dealt with her own medical issues related to a horrible care accident she suffered a year or two before. She was a flight nurse and had crashed en route to work. She had to be manually extricated and was saved by some passersby before her vehicle burst into flames. She had been through a very difficult time—multiple injuries and multiple surgeries and continued pain. She was still using crutches and such.

Jess was a lifelong friend and classmate of mine; she had been a great friend to me, especially after my divorce so many years ago. She opened her home to me during holidays when I might otherwise have been all alone. In summer and fall, She and Sky and I would sit and have garage beers, along with Sky's husband, Montana. I always looked forward to those days. It was usually after one of us had a particularly shitty day, someone would start the text string "garage beers, 6 p.m."

Jess had befriended Jan while they were both attending New Mexico Junior College in Hobbs, New Mexico, after they each graduated high school. Jan grew up in a small West Texas town not too far from Lovington. Originally from Welch, Texas, she later graduated from Denver City High. Jess and Jan had remained friends into adulthood, and it was during one visit to Lovington, years after we were both divorced, that I finally got to meet Jan. She was in town visiting Jess, and she ended up making her way out to a local golf tournament I was playing in. Jess and Sky had told me stories about her and shown me pictures of her. She was a beauty, and Jess and Sky both swore she was one of the sweetest girls they had ever met. That was saying a lot. Jess and Jan would tell crazy but innocent stories about going to school, drinking beer and living life.

I hadn't seen Jess or Sky since my death. We had texted; they checked on me often, but there had been no face-to-face time. When we arrived at Jess's house, the hugs were on in full force—Jess and her kids—her mom even came over. It was great to see them. Sky and I had grown close during my time working in Lovington, more than five years before my heart attack. She and her husband, Montana, were great friends to me; we all spent a lot of time together after my divorce and before I met Jan. Sky and I also worked together in the Lovington emergency room a few years before her jump in to flight nursing. As Sky arrived to see us, it became a bit more emotional, but we were all strong and just happy to see each other. I, of course, was happy to be seen by anyone!

And so the ER shifts in Lovington came and went without incident. The old workflow quickly fell in place; thankfully, there had not yet been a COVID surge in this area, so the ER wasn't too busy. I had time to run to the medical clinics, which were connected to the hospital via long hallways, and see my old friends working in the clinic.

Everyone was so kind, so many stories of prayer chains and good thoughts coming my way. They always made me feel special here. I made my way to the CEO's office. He had taken the time to text and offer words of encouragement when I was released from the hospital. Jess, who now worked at the hospital in Lovington, had relayed how the CEO had placed me on his prayer groups list. I was so struck by the kindness of the people in this small town. I wanted to shake his hand and thank him or maybe give him a fist bump. He had also allowed me to return to cover the shifts in the ER. I felt that was a particularly nice gesture, given what I had been through.

I was told so many stories about my hometown rallying around me from afar. There were high school alumni chat pages where many of my old classmates raised me up in prayer, offered words of encouragement, most of whom I hadn't been in contact with since we left high school. Yet in my time of need, the Wildcats rallied up support.

Really, the only negative of my post-heart-attack return to Lovington was that my former clinic medical assistant Norma, who previously made bizcochitos when I came in to town to work, no longer offered them. Those were no longer on my diet. Damn!

And so, post shift, Jan and I returned to our hotel. I showered, and we prepared for a short hour and a half trek across the state line to Lubbock. It was my birthday weekend, and we were going to spend at least the first part of it with my best buddy from medical school and his family. I was excited to see him. He had been a pillar of support to Jan and the kids with medical advice and insight and of course, per his new hobby, had type written me letters of support.

CHAPTER 7

BIRTHDAY

Joe and I became friends toward the end of medical school. He was from Bloomfield, New Mexico, had attended the University of New Mexico, and then, like me, was admitted to the University of New Mexico school of medicine. We were friendly throughout medical school and even played golf together here and there; we were similar cats. He, however, was a more outspoken, intelligent, and articulate soul. He could offer up a well-thought-out soliloquy or simply string together a series of insults and cuss words that always made me weak with laughter.

We became close during our fourth and final year of medical school. It was during this fateful time that I decided to pursue a residency in neurosurgery. It is generally in the fourth year that medical students start to consider what specialty to purse and plan their year and month-long clinical rotations accordingly. Early in my fourth year, I had been on the search for a replacement clinical rotation, as the primary care rotation that I had signed up for had been canceled for some reason. So I decided I would try a month-long rotation in a specialty that I would likely never get to experience; I chose neurosurgery.

I figured the residents would let me follow them around and see things that I may never get to see again. I had always enjoyed the pomp and circumstance of the operating room, from the seemingly strict rules governing who came in the room to the attention to detail of scrubbing each of your fingers on both sides and under your fingernails before walking in to dry off and have your gloves placed on your hands. There were a number of rules about how long to scrub your hands clean prior to entering the room. The one that stuck with me as a medical student at the time was to scrub longer than anyone senior to you who was scrubbing in for the surgery. So as a medical student who was essentially everyone from interns, residents to, of course, attending physicians, you just kept scrubbing until every else stopped and made their way into the operating you.

It was a great month; the residents took a liking to me and made it a great experience. They allowed me to follow them, scrubbing into as many cases as I could get in. They took the time to teach me about CT scan findings and specific neurologic clinical findings that I might not otherwise learn.

Over the course of the month, I fell in love with the idea of being a neurosurgeon but had no idea about how to go about it. I researched, and I jumped in with both feet. As I came to find out, those students going into neurosurgery are a relatively small group, and there are even fewer neurosurgery residency positions to be had by these applicants.

Joe, of course, knew he wanted to be a neurosurgeon much earlier in the course of medical school and had taken all the proper steps, including lighting up the board exams, which are used to help determine your worthiness in obtaining a residency spot. One day, during our fourth year, Joe called me out of the blue. It was time to submit our match list for residencies, and he wanted to feel me out. He was, as always, a gentleman, direct and articulate in where he stood. I can remember distinctly his words: "I mean, I know you. I like you, and I don't want to go out of my way to try to fuck you over just to get a residency spot. That being said, I wanted you to know, I am ranking UNM on my list."

I laughed at the directness, but it was refreshing. I explained to Joe, UNM would also be high on my list as well and would have to be at the very top, as it was my only real chance of winning a residency spot. I explained that I imagined his board scores and medical school transcripts were better than mine, and I didn't really have the hardcore externships and letters that a typical medical student seeking a neurosurgery residency position might have. That said, I had rotated at UT Southwestern, a very well-known program with a very well-known chairman, Dr. Duke Samson. Joe and I used to joke that Dr. Samson even looked mean in his bio pic online! I had a great but somewhat limited experience with Dr. Samson; he had told me I had done well in my short time as a visiting medical student, and he thought I was a good candidate. That was like career gold!

And so it was, Joe and I put it all on the line for each other. There was only one candidate accepted into the UNM neurosurgery residency program. We weren't going to undermine the other; we were simply going to put our best foot forward, and the better man would win. And with that, we earned each other's respect and trust. I certainly hoped I would get it but wanted Joe to get it if I didn't.

On match day, we celebrated together. I had matched at UNM, and Joe, of course, had earned a more prestigious neurosurgery position at Baylor. We raised a glass together. Our friendship would flourish from there. We had remained friends long distance through residency, supporting each other through the dark days of internship and residency. I offered words of support to him through his divorce and then him to me through mine. I was disappointed to inform him the day I told him I was leaving neurosurgery residency and switching specialties, yet no one could understand better than him. He only offered his support.

We had a mountain of memories together. While Joe was still in residency and after he was divorced, he would come to New Mexico for one of his vacation weeks, as it was inexpensive, and we could golf every day. One particular time, after I started working in Lovington, Joe came to town; we made it out to the golf course for a couple of days of golfing, telling stories, and drinking beer. Once we were done golfing for the day, we were set on having Mexican food and taking it to my house for us and my family. Joe began to order and didn't stop till we had just about one of every combination on the menu. In his drunkenness and apparent hunger state, he considered everything that might taste good and added it to our order. We left the restaurant with our arms full of carryout bags. We made it home, ate a few bites, and passed out.

Later, after Joe had completed residency and started his first job in Miami and after I was divorced, he and I met up for a golf trip. We stayed at a lush resort in Palm Beach. We decided we were going to golf all day. It was warm and sticky out, perfect for drinking and golfing. We proceeded to finish our first round and decided to make use of the phenomenal facilities in the locker room and shower up for lunch. We bought new clothes in the pro shop and, feeling like we looked our best, sat for lunch and some cape cods. Joe somehow pieced together some salmon-colored shorts with fish or seahorses on them and an equally loud white-and-blue golf shirt. I managed to find something a bit more traditional.

We then, for some reason, actually went out to try and play eighteen more holes. We made it through about four holes. I don't particularly remember how we were playing, but I know we had fun. We were sloshed. We took the golf cart off road. We crossed a busy street and drove the cart to the beach. We thought we were the funniest guys alive. Somehow, we made it back to the course to be driven back to the hotel in time to get ready for dinner, I think. It was pretty downhill from there. We always took great pics of our adventures, so it was easy to scroll through my phone later and let out a chuckle at the thoughts of our good times.

Jan and I were pulling up to Joe's house in Lubbock. He had a beautiful huge home. He came out to meet us. I gave him a big hug. He gave me a huge hug back. I couldn't help the tears that were flowing. We embraced for a few minutes. We were both speechless. It was good to be alive.

As per routine, Joe poured up the champagne, along with Jan and Joe's wife, Rikki. We toasted being alive and proceeded to plan a phenomenal evening. The following day was my birthday, and we would be driving back to Las Cruces to share the evening with our family, but for tonight, we were celebrating with good friends. So we went to a very nice dinner, after which, it struck Joe: we needed to celebrate some more. We went to a hip wine bar. Joe managed to research and find us a one-hundred-point wine. It was my birthday, dammit, and we were having one-hundred-point wine, which neither of us had ever had before. Joe found the one, a bottle of Vecina 2016 Cabernet Sauvignon. I tried to convince him that such extravagance wasn't necessary and insisted he let me help pay for the bottle, to no avail. "You died, bro!" he yelled. And so it was, a great evening, a great bottle of wine (or a couple), and a great time with wonderful friends. Life was indeed good.

I hadn't been drunk and, therefore, not hungover for months, so I was not too pleasantly awakened with a mild headache and feeling of dehydration the following morning. Yet I was happy. I had survived to see another birthday. Joe and Rikki went out of their way with birthday gifts; their kids had made me a birthday cake the night prior while we were out to dinner. Great kids! We toasted with cake, we sang happy birthday and blew out the candles, and we celebrated, and then, Jan and I were on our way home.

By the time we arrived in Las Cruces, Jan and I were more alive and feeling good. I was glad to be home, celebrating with family. Anna and Luke wrote me great and very personal birthday cards. It was evident the reins were off; we would just share our open minds. What could be greater? Shelby called in long distance from Dallas; we missed her. Jan, as always, made it a memorable day, and we both shed a tear at being able to celebrate this milestone together. So many tears nowadays.

CHAPTER 8

BILLS AND FINANCES

It was along this time that I began to receive bills in full force. The number of bills and the number of different sources of bills were mind-numbing. I worked in medicine and allegedly knew how the system worked, yet Jan and I were overwhelmed by the volume of mail. As people apparently experience every day, when you visit the ER emergently and get admitted to the hospital, you get bills from the ER staffing company, you get a bill from the hospital itself, you get billed by the hospitalist staffing company, you get billed by each individual specialist (the infectious disease doc, the pulmonary critical care doc, the cardiology doc), the home oxygen company, the life vest company, and on and on. All told the bill was almost five hundred thousand dollars.

I ignored the mountain of bills. I would get to it in the following months once we had steady income coming in, and I could make good faith attempts to pay cash for any services. How did people do it? How do you know which bill to pay and which can wait? Thankfully, insurance took care of most of the bill. Nonetheless, there were tens of thousands of dollars' worth of bills collecting in the corner. How did people do it?

How do people with no knowledge of medicine or medical billing do it? How do they keep from getting overwhelmed? How do they know when to start paying and not pay a bill that later changes to paid after insurance covers it? How does anyone know? Is this billing method intentionally confusing? Do insurance companies take advantage of those less knowledgeable souls?

I became angry. Why did it have to be so difficult? And so into the pile each bill went. I paid the small ones and set out a plan to try to tackle the big ones. Funds were limited; we had no way to pay all the bills and pay our usual monthly bills and still keep our heads above water for very long.

As Jan and I continued our shared efforts in monitoring finances, it became abundantly clear our savings wouldn't last another three to four months if we were going to also begin paying the mounting bills. We had planned out our savings and trade accounts and figured conservatively, if we didn't earn another dollar, we could live for six months. We felt comfortable with that cushion, given my clinical improvement, but we needed to start generating some income. I hadn't received a full paycheck in a couple of months; the partial shifts and Lovington ER shifts were helpful but far from what we typically had coming in and certainly not enough alone to cover our monthly expenses.

Then I got a phone call. My ER employers called to tell me any future shifts were on hold. The chief executive officer of the hospital wanted to meet with me to discuss my work status. "Why does he want to meet? I've been released by my cardiologist," I explained to the ER company vice president, who initiated the call.

"I think the hospital just wants to be sure you are safe to return, and they want to discuss that with you themselves," he replied. "The CEO's secretary will contact you and set up a meeting."

"Okay, thanks," I replied.

"What the hell?" I muttered to myself. I worked hard not to let my imagination run wild. What was going on? Maybe they just want to see me for themselves and make sure I'm fully intact and review my records to be sure everything is in order with regard to work release notes and my PT, OT, and speech-language evaluations, but isn't that the role of my employer, the ER staffing company?

My new work position was a weird circumstance in that I didn't really work for the hospital itself. That is to say, I wasn't a hospital employee. I was employed by the ER staffing company that had the

ER contract at the hospital. I had worked for the hospital itself as the urgent care clinics director, and they allowed me to work in the ER part-time for whichever company had the ER contract at the time. I had decided to leave my hospital-based position with the urgent care and commit to the ER full-time earlier in the year and approximately three months before my MI.

So my ER company was telling me the hospital CEO wanted to meet with me. It was the equivalent of a house painter working for a subcontractor being called into the main contractor's office for a discussion and evaluation. It didn't make a lot of sense to me, but then, what I had been through was itself an unusual circumstance, and I was certainly willing to do whatever it took to be in the good graces of all involved and get back to work as soon as possible. I felt that if my treating physician said I was okay to work and my employer was allowing me to come back to work, what concern would the CEO have about all of it?

Nonetheless, the meeting was scheduled, and I showed up as requested. The CEO wasn't particularly warm; he had never reached out that I was aware of during my illness and certainly hadn't texted like the previous CEO. I hadn't developed the relationship with him, while I was still working at urgent care that I had with his predecessor, who had hired me. He proceeded to lay out in a very pragmatic fashion that hospital policy is such that any physician that has a major medical event must undergo a review by a group of his peers, an ad hoc committee named the wellness committee. They were charged with making sure any physician who had recovered from a serious medical event was indeed in proper working order and capable of delivering the standard of care in a manner that was safe for patients. It seemed reasonable to me, and since the CEO said it was routine, I eagerly agreed and offered to meet with the committee asap.

I don't know why I thought of it at the time, but I wondered if I should ask about the promotion I was promised if I agreed to go to the ER full-time way back at the beginning of the year. I thought, why not? So it came out of my mouth. "Do you mind if I ask why I wasn't made the ER director, as was previously discussed?"

He was taken aback. I could see his eyes moving side to side, searching for the proper answer. So I offered, "I don't mean to catch you off guard, but I was never really told why that never happened."

"Well, you aren't board certified in emergency medicine. You didn't meet the qualifications for the jobs," he stated, matter-of-factly.

I was incredulous. I had gone through great lengths and spent lots of time and energy putting together a plan to become board certified and provided this plan to all the credentialing committees and hospital boards and medical executive committees for approval, and I had fully and wholly received that approval—and all with the assistance from administrative managers associated with the very office I was sitting in. I started to become angry but managed to remain outwardly calm and reminded myself to be gentlemanly and courteous in the professional setting. "Well, I submitted my plan to become certified, and it was approved by the board, yet I was told by my employer that the hospital administration wanted another candidate. The only reason I left my director position with the urgent care clinics was to take over the ER director position, and I was told it was mine to have before I ever agreed to leave my prior position," I shared by way of trying to politely disprove his statement.

"Well, you weren't told that by me!" he retorted.

It was apparent this was not going to be helpful to me, so I simply thanked him for his time and agreed to meet with the ad hoc committee when they were ready. "If it's possible, could you request the committee meet with me as soon as possible. I would like to complete all necessary requirements so I can get on the ER schedule as soon as possible this month, as I'm quickly approaching a financial crisis since I've had no full-time income for a few months now," I requested. He assured me he would get with the chair of the newly formed committee and have them expedite my meeting.

I left there proud of myself for asking the tough question but growing more confused about what had happened to the position promised to me at the beginning of the year. The ER staffing company I worked for had said the administration wanted an outside candidate. When I had queried the administration at the time, they indicated this was fully the decision of the ER staffing company.

Still, it didn't make any sense; clearly, one of the parties wasn't being honest.

I was also very uneasy about the ad hoc committee. What would they require of me to return to work? Surely, they would read my work release notes from my cardiologist, who was on staff at the same hospital. The CEO mentioned they might want more proof of my fitness to work. What else could they want? *Oh,* I thought to myself, *they probably want to see my PT, OT, and speech-language therapist's evaluations, and they likely want to ask me a few questions and see with their own eyes that I am really okay.* I reasoned it must be difficult for them to know my true status without talking to me!

I started to prepare all the documentation I had about my hospitalization, rehabilitation, and the multiple evaluations I had undergone to prove my fitness to return to work. I was ready to send them at a moment's notice. And so I waited for their call, but the call did not come quickly from the committee.

A week later, I e-mailed the CEO to see if I could get an update on the committee, as I was anxious to get it done, and so much time had passed. The committee would be meeting very soon, I was assured. Later in that week, I received an e-mail. The committee had indeed met and requested a neuropsychiatric exam be performed before I would be granted full release to return to work. "What the hell are they talking about?" I said aloud.

Jan was near me and said, "What's wrong?" The committee wants me to have a specific independent medical evaluation to be assured there were no neurologic sequelae from the cardiac event I suffered. I was flabbergasted; they must be confused. They haven't even talked to me or interviewed me. How did they arrive at this decision? Did they review my hospital medical record? They hadn't requested anything from me!

I grew angry and fearful. What was happening here? Getting any type of specialty exam would take months to get done. Then to have the results sent back to the committee then possibly released to work, we were talking at least two to three months, at best! How were we going to make that work financially? We had to figure something out quickly.

I started shooting off e-mails to the hospital CEO, copying the administrative liaison, who was my connection to the ad hoc committee, with whom I had yet to meet. I asked the obvious questions: Why was this requested? Did the committee misunderstand and think I had a stroke instead of a heart attack? Would they like to see all my release notes and therapy evaluations?

I received prompt e-mail replies. The committee had not reviewed any records; they did not have access to them. They were following hospital policy in requesting this next step. The administrative liaison would be happy to help me find a facility, in which the neuropsychiatric exam could be performed. The CEO indicated he was happy to meet with me again to discuss any questions, but the committee worked independently of the CEO; he had no say in what was requested.

The liaison informed me the committee would be happy to meet with me in person, if I liked, to explain their reasoning and the hospital bylaws by which they were working. *Hell, yes,* I thought to myself as I read the reply e-mails. I want to sit in front of these people and see what their concerns are and explain my current status. They truly have no idea I have been restored.

CHAPTER 9

GRADUATING, 5K

I continued to go to rehab because I enjoyed the exercise and also because it became apparent that I needed to cross every T and dot every I. I needed to complete this course and get the certificate of completion to demonstrate my cardiac fitness. I was waiting to meet with the committee; they had scheduled a sit-down, in-person meeting with me in a couple of weeks. In the interim, I kept busy with exercise and studying. Jan and I were still working on our ability to run a 5K. We would run/walk a 5K once a week, while I also attended cardiac rehab, and we would fill our fifth day of exercise with something fun: a hike, riding bikes, tennis—whatever we could manage.

The final couple of cardiac rehab sessions had arrived. By this time, I was working out harder outside of cardiac rehab, but I still enjoyed working out inside the air-conditioned rehab building and talking to the nurses and getting updates on the goings on at the hospital. They were always encouraging and often asked when I would be returning to the ER. I only shared that more evaluations were requested by the hospital. "Why? You're doing great here. Do they need my notes to prove it?" the rehab nurse offered.

"I don't know, I guess they just want to give me a hard time," I would reply.

The final cardiac rehab session arrived. I was happy to be completing this aspect as it represented the final hurdle over which to jump and confirm I was healthy and rehabilitated—restored, as we came to say. The whole idea of being restored started with a friend of my mother-in-law. She was one of the great prayer warriors that my mother-in-law had been friends with for a number of years; she had sent cards and meals during my recovery. One afternoon, Jan and I were finishing up thank you notes and then going to mail them out when we decided we would deliver her thank you note in person.

As we drove into her neighborhood, we saw her dusting off her car outside her garage. We pulled up, and I stepped out of the car. She took one look at me. "Oh my god, He has restored you!" she almost screamed. "Oh, *mijo*, you look so good." We thanked her profusely, and we later recounted how she had specifically used the term "restored." I decided I would use it every chance I got, not in a braggadocios sense but in a true testament to God's power to heal. Okay, yes, also to brag! I felt I earned it. We adopted the Bible verse 1 Peter 5:10 as our new life verse.

And so the final day of cardiac rehab had arrived. I excitedly completed each exercise station that day and, as always, exercised longer or did more repetitions than was assigned. I finished my last stretching exercise. I was done! The nurses congratulated me and had a certificate and a T-shirt for me! To my surprise, in walked my wife and kids. Jan, Luke, and Anna came in with balloons, a small trophy, and breakfast snacks for the nurses. We took celebratory pictures, and we thanked them for supporting me and helping me to heal. They had helped me build my confidence, both in my physical abilities and my mental strength, whether they knew it or not.

On the ride home, I was all smiles, music turned up, windows rolled down. Jan and the kids were in Jan's car, and we pulled into the driveway at home together. Jan and Anna let Luke out of the car and decided they would go get us some food to eat. Jan said again how proud she was of me. For whatever reason, it made me feel so happy and accomplished. The tears started to flow. I gave her a hug through her car window before they drove off. I guess it felt like somewhat of a weight being lifted. Although that day was no different from the day before, I was in the same physical condition, formally announcing I had completed rehab was a great milestone.

The completion of cardiac rehab had a significant impact on my outlook. I could look at that accomplishment and know I had recovered fully cardiovascularly. If I had a twinge of chest pain that began to be of concern to me, I would reason that I had made it through rehab, at times pushing myself as hard as I have at any time, and there were no arrhythmias, no evidence of ischemia. In short, I could do anything physically now because I had the comfort of knowing I had done it before without issue. It had a great impact on my confidence and my mental strength going forward. Also, as I had hoped, it marked the completion of my recovery, at least in a formal sense and was the final check mark on my list to return to work and life in general. I was back. I was restored!

Jan and I continued to run and walk and bike for exercise. We were improving our conditioning and really running well for a large portion of a 5K. We drove out to the north side of town to the Redhawk Golf Club and parked and ran and walked down the paved sidewalk paths leading up and down the main road into the club. It was nice and reasonably flat area, which was in stark contrast to our very hilly neighborhood, which was a different kind of running challenge. Since we would be running our 5K in downtown Dallas, we figured we could at least train on a somewhat flat surface; with the gain in elevation, we felt we would potentially perform even better in the city. We couldn't wait for the day of the race; training was getting monotonous.

We really built up the importance of the 5K. In retrospect, the training gave us a focus while life seemed to fall down around us, with work on hold, medical bills stacking up, an ongoing pandemic. It provided us a healthy way to be outdoors together, each of us pounding the pavement on a course new to us. I believe it also gave us something to focus on that wasn't the fear and pain we had lived through. For me, running a 5K, similar to the completion of cardiac rehab, was a grander, more outwardly visible expression of my recovery of our survival and verification of the hard work we put in over the course of multiple months. We wanted to run the 5K in downtown Dallas for the dramatic backdrop and exciting and busy environment in which to complete our race. The race was actually virtual; again, due to COVID, it would be different from the traditional format. It was our first, so we had no expectations. We just knew we wanted to beat our training times. I couldn't wait to stand there sweaty and catching my breath, with my arm held high in the air, victorious, restored for all to see.

We planned to run the race there, then celebrate Thanksgiving with all the family together. It was the first time we would get to see Shelby since she left after I got home from the hospital. It was the perfect plan; we just had to do our part and keep training so as not to embarrass ourselves.

It was about this time that some of my ER colleagues—a PA and a nurse—texted and asked if they could come by to see us and say hello. I was excited to hear from them and, of course, said yes to their visit. We had had a few friends and neighbors come visit since I had been home and many others who had indicated they would as soon as it was safe. Of course, my brother and his family, our good friends Jeremiah and Veronica, and our neighbors Brian and Nancy had come by. My parents had been by a couple of times.

They came by one hot afternoon, bearing gifts: a plant, a card, and a bottle of scotch. Joanna, the ER charge nurse who was on duty the day I came in, dated a former colleague of ours who was roommates with Shawn, who was a PA in the ER. Shawn relayed all the goings on at the ER. He said I was fortunate to not be working now; things were busy and, in fact, overwhelming during the pandemic.

Joanna informed us she no long worked in the ER. She had moved on to another opportunity. She said that the events of my visit to the ER had affected her, and she no longer found the extreme stress and overwhelming nature of our ER appealing. I felt bad for her; she was a very kind and smart young nurse. Although somewhat hesitant, I proceeded to ask her about the details of my ER visit. Jan had filled me in from her perspective, but I had not really had the chance to ask anyone who was there that day about the clinical aspects, which is a little weird given how much time had passed, but then I guess most patients don't readily ask or know to ask about clinical specifics of their visits.

Joanna began to tell an unbelievable story. After I had arrived and initially was awake and talking, I had a sudden cardiac arrhythmia and passed out. She said they couldn't feel a pulse and started screaming, "Oh, shit, I don't feel a pulse. Start CPR and call the doc!" She said she and the nurses present initiated CPR until the ER doc arrived, and they continued for an extended period and could not seem to gain a sustainable pulse or a shockable rhythm.

After an extended course, they checked rhythm and got a shockable rhythm, ventricular fibrillation, and shocked me out of it. They intubated me. I appeared to be stabilizing, but then a few minutes later—again, pulseless electrical activity—CPR was started. The cycle started again, and so it went until they again regained a pulse. They called in the cardiologist, and in the midst of waiting, I coded a third time. It was during this time that Jan and the kids and my brother were in the waiting room, hearing the code blue calls but not knowing, the full magnitude of what was happening until the moment the nurse manager and the social worker went out together to bring Jan in to see me undergoing CPR.

Joanna relayed they didn't know how long to keep going. After Jan saw me and left the room, they continued; there was discussion about cessation of resuscitative efforts if I didn't respond shortly; it had been almost an hour. Joanna said she and a couple of nurses spoke out against stopping and recommended continuing all efforts. "It's Dr. Acosta. He can't die!" she quoted someone as saying. They continued and ultimately found a rhythm, cleared, and shock delivered. I stabilized. It was then that I was rushed out to the cardiac catheterization lab. She said it was chaos; they were emotionally drained; the trauma room was a disaster. It was then that the nurses gathered to pray. I was in tears when she finished. All I could manage was a thank you.

We steered the conversation to lighter topics, and they soon said their goodbyes, and we promised to get together again to open the scotch. Jan and I hugged when they left. "Are you okay?" she asked.

"Yes. It's just a lot, you know?" I said.

It was indeed a lot. It prompted me to look into survival rates for patients suffering multiple cardiac arrests. The best I could find was a study that quoted rates for hospitalized patients who suffered multiple cardia arrests and survived to be discharged from the hospital. Survival percentage: 7.9 percent.[1] I shared it with Jan. "I knew you were a miracle," she said. Restored indeed.

---

[1] Long-term survival after successful inhospital cardiac arrest resuscitation (*American Heart Journal*, May 2007).

CHAPTER 10

LOSING A JOB

A few days before my scheduled meeting with the hospital wellness committee, I received a certified letter from the committee; it was a response to my previous e-mail questioning the necessity of neuropsychiatric exam. It started with the corporate speak about hospital bylaws and protocols to follow in circumstances such as this, and it ended with "this committee is acting in response to concerns brought to our attention solely by your employer."

"You have absolutely got to be fucking kidding me!" I yelled at no one.

Jan heard. "What happened?"

"You're not going to believe this!" I said loudly, essentially yelling. The ER company is the one that initiated this entire wellness committee fiasco. I was not surprised in the least; it had been one lie after another with them, and it was becoming all too clear what was happening. It also laid bare the CEO's words that this was a typical and standard process for physicians recovering from illness. The hospital bylaws themselves, which were included with the certified mail, stated specifically, a committee would be formed in response to any concern raised about a physician's ability to perform standard clinical duties.

Days later, and coincidentally just one day before my scheduled meeting with the wellness committee, I received a text from the ER company regional VP. He requested a phone conference that evening. Likely figuring I had nothing going on since I wasn't allowed to return to work, he offered a specific conference time, to which I agreed since I had nothing going on.

Jan and I prepared for the meeting. We were going to record and document. We ran through the plan; we practiced the questions; we would put them on the spot now that we knew they were responsible for the wellness committee. My cell phone rang at the scheduled time. There were the usual welcoming pleasantries. I was informed there were two others on the call from the ER company. They noted that they were very happy for me and had offered their support of me in my recovery. They noted that they hadn't reached out due to the difficulty of communicating during my illness and because the pandemic limited any visitation in the hospital. My wife and I rolled our eyes at each other quietly; so many others had managed to reach out and get in touch, and they weren't my employer, but so be it.

They started with their concerns. During my brief return to work, the half shifts, they noted that I appeared fatigued and I had indicated that I was tired to the nursing staff. "Well, yes, I did get tired working. I just had a heart attack, but I was able to perform my duties, and I said I was tired after my shifts, not during. But now it's more than a month later, and I've completed cardiac rehab, and my wife and I are training for a 5K, so stamina isn't really an issue," I replied. Jan nodded supportively. We nailed that one!

They also had concerns about some of my clinical charting at work and my clinical diagnoses; a couple of random charts were reviewed, and one of the ER patients I had seen had returned with the same symptoms days later, and two others, although technically appropriately diagnosed, didn't have documentation of possible alternative diagnosis and didn't receive all the medication they could have received. There had been no complications, but they were concerned that maybe my stamina was keeping me from developing a full differential diagnosis and therapeutic regimen. "Well, it's a little hard to speak to those specific cases on the spot without being provided the clinical chart and time to review, but I don't remember being notified of any complications or called with concerns by any patient or any of the consulting physicians or hospitalist. And as I remember it, since it was the freestanding ER, not all of the medications you mentioned that were allegedly not ordered are not available there. There is a limited pharmacy formulary as compared to the main ER," I retorted.

They proceeded to tell me that collectively, they were concerned these perceived shortcomings were all the result of my no longer having the stamina to perform the work of an emergency room physician. They felt it best that we part ways. They could, of course, provide me with some measure of severance pay if I would agree to the terms by the end of the week. My jaw dropped. Jan's eyes began to well with tears. "Um, I'm not sure what to say. I didn't expect to be fired today. In fact, I've never been fired in my life," I managed to get out.

How could this be happening? Just seven months prior, they were preparing me to take over as director, and now they wanted me gone? What? It didn't make sense! What happened? They had no more answers; they had done what they set out to do during this phone call. The current regional medical ER director, who was on the call, and the one who had made all the false promises wanted us to be sure we knew it was tough and awkward for her too. She was sorry this tough conversation had to happen. Screw you!

Jan and I sat in disbelief after the phone call had ended. What do we do now? Did we need to consider bankruptcy? Was I really done working in the ER? *What happened?* How did it all come to this? All the while, the regional medical ER director was texting. She wanted to explain. "Please call me," she pleaded in her text. What a vile, conniving bitch she turned out to be. I was amazed that this was a professional organization.

We struggled with answers and, in our own ways, mentally tried to make sense of it all. We immediately had the idea and mentality that we were going to sue. We wouldn't let them mistreat us and take advantage of me while I was down. We would find the best lawyers, and we would make them pay. We sat there together the rest of the evening in complete disbelief at how things had transpired until it was time for bed.

The following day, we performed our usual routine: cup of decaf, *Today* show, stock market, exercise, and then a healthy lunch.

We were going to go to church that night, a Wednesday, not part of our usual routine, but given the events of the past day, we thought it a good variation from our routine. It was also the day of the scheduled meeting with the wellness committee, which we had previously been anxiously awaiting. *But what was the use now?* we wondered. There appeared to be no benefit of having the meeting. Maybe I would call and cancel. We discussed it and thought we don't feel we've been given all the necessary information as to how we got here; maybe we should go and see what information we can gain.

We decided we were going to walk in with our heads held high and inform the committee of the ER companies request for my resignation. We would make them look us in the eye and tell us why they helped make this happen, then we would be off to church and maybe an evening glass of wine. We talked through the possible directions the meeting might go. At this point, we were hypervigilant; we needed to be prepared for anything and be able to respond accordingly. We also wanted to be prepared to ask more questions; we were after all, going to sue everyone.

We dressed and made the short drive to the hospital for the meeting, which was scheduled in the administrative conference room on the first floor of the main hospital. In order to limit exposures during COVID, they asked that we wear masks, and Jan would have to wait alone in a waiting area while I went into the conference room. In the conference room, we were all seated six feet apart; only two of the four medical staff committee members were able to attend, along with the administrative liaison.

They opened the meeting by thanking me for coming in and with words of support for my recovery from the MI. They then began citing again the hospital bylaws that required the committee to be formed. They relayed that they had received very specific concerns from the ER medical director and also had spoken to a couple of the physicians with whom I performed my half shifts. They noted that the ER regional medical director cited stamina as an issue, and one of the ER docs, my colleague, had also mentioned I had said I was getting tired after the modified shift. Therefore, they would continue to recommend the neuropsychiatric exam otherwise referred to as an independent medical exam, as had been previously documented.

"Thank you for explaining your thought process to me. Now that I'm aware that the concerns were raised by my employer—and specifically the ER director, who is my immediate supervisor—it has become clear to me what has happened," I started, "But before I share with you my opinion about why this has become an issue for this committee to consider, I feel compelled to let you know that the ER company contacted me yesterday and asked that I resign, or I would be fired."

Silence. If not for the requisite mask, I'm sure visible evidence of jaws dropping would have occurred. "Dr. Acosta, we were not aware of that. I'm sorry," one of the docs said.

"Thank you, and I'm sorry to come in here and drop this on you, but rather than discuss in detail why I don't feel a neuropsych exam is necessary, I thought I would let you know that any discussion is essentially moot since I won't be working in your ER anymore," I shared. "I'm sorry for my e-mails protesting your recommendation. I had no idea my employer brought the issues to you in the first place. Obviously, I would have replied differently if I had known there were any concerns raised. I'm sorry they never discussed those concerns with me directly until last night when they fired me.

"Furthermore, the more I think about it, the more I'm of the opinion that it was a coordinated effort by them. They asked me to join the ER staff full-time with the promise of becoming the ER director, and when they couldn't get that plan approved by hospital administration, I became a liability as I would surely raise a stink about giving up a director position to come to the ER. So it was convenient that I fell ill. They then were able to raise these concerns to you without informing me so that you would officially document those concerns, and I'd be pushed into a corner to comply, and they could then ask me to resign due to their concerns and the alleged lack of compliance with the committee request for exam, never mind they never gave me the opportunity or time to comply."

As I finished, the emotions came forward. I didn't fully get the last of the sentence out before I had to stop to squelch any breakdown. The committee was moved; they apologized profusely and offered to help me in any way possible. One of the docs was so moved, he reached out to me privately the day after the meeting via e-mail to offer his support.

I did think to ask the committee which doctors they spoke to regarding my half shift performance. They generalized and said most of the docs they spoke with said I did fine, but one or two of them noted that I seemed tired. I asked if they could tell me which doctors those were since I would no longer be working there, and they were now largely responsible for my loss of employment. They shared the name, and it was no surprise. With coworkers like him, who needed enemies?

I thanked the committee for their time and for considering my health in their deliberations and for taking the time to sit with me and explain the details. We adjourned, and I walked out to find Jan. She was anxious to hear all about it, particularly since the meeting lasted a full fifteen minutes. So we walked to our car and began our drive to church. I told her of the medical director's concerns and the doctor who threw me under the bus. It was no surprise to her either. "What a backstabbing piece of crap!" she snarled.

"I know," I agreed. "If he only knew what we knew about him and his checkered past, he might have reconsidered his self-indulgent assessments." I thought for a minute I should call him.

Jan resisted the idea. "Why don't you give it some time?" she recommended.

"I don't know that time is going to change how I feel about him sharing any opinion that he didn't even discuss with me," I argued.

"Well, you're probably right, but let's just wait." Jan could get just as fiery as I could under the right circumstances, but she was certainly correct in this moment. "Maybe they didn't tell him they were going to share his opinions with you?" she offered by way of considering both sides of the problem.

"Well, I don't know why he would think different. I'm sure the committee called and said who they were and why they wanted the information. If someone called and asked me about it, I would be honest, but I would also let the person I was asked about know what

70

I said just as a courtesy. Don't you think you would?" I replied, primarily thinking out loud.

I couldn't stand not doing something, so I settled for a text. "Hi, I hope you are well. I was told by the wellness committee of your negative review of my time working with you. I would have appreciated a heads up from you regarding your feelings. The ER company has asked that I resign," I texted.

Jan and I continued to drive. By the time we walked into church, we received no reply. We never would.

CHAPTER 11

HOLIDAYS

Jan and I went back and forth, discussing the possibility of filing a lawsuit against the ER company. We consulted our good friend, a newly retired malpractice attorney. He offered his views but more than that asked that I consider how this might all ultimately affect me. If a suit was filed, it would likely include the hospital as a defendant in a small city; cutting your work opportunities by 50 percent was not necessarily a good move. He asked, what if I got labeled a "troublemaker"? Certainly, that would follow me likely throughout the state and region. He asked if I was prepared to deal with that.

He was a great medical malpractice attorney; his parents were both physicians, so he did the natural thing and went into law. He always amused me with his medical knowledge. And it wasn't just the strict medical terms and procedures; he understood the nuance and spoke like a doctor. I never met another med-mal attorney like him. Thankfully, I never really had to meet many; nonetheless, he seemed to be a rarity.

His particular insight was great. In spite of his warnings of the negative outcomes, he felt I had a reasonably strong case and recommended I speak to a labor and employment attorney. Jan and I discussed the possibilities; we weren't going to sign the severance deal. The deadline to return the severance offer came and went. We were determined to fight.

The ER regional VP texted a day or two after the deadline and asked if I had planned to accept the terms offered. "No, I don't feel that is fair to me," I replied. He asked what I felt might be fair, essentially opening a discussion as to how much money it was going to take to go away. I arrogantly and angrily retorted with an amount. He would be in touch.

He did indeed get in touch. He asked if he could set up another phone conference with me. Sure, I said. I would be prepared to share specifics to try and sway him about the severance deal, I thought. He informed me that he wanted set up a phone conference with the CMO. The CMO? I wondered what good that was, likely a plan to strong-arm me into signing the deal. The phone call turned out to be more of the same: "We're on your side," "We know it is unfair that you got sick," "We're happy to help you with new opportunities," "We think you're an awesome provider. You're just not what we need in the ER right now," blah, blah, blah.

Okay, I said. I would get back to them. They set a deadline to hear back and requested that I send the original severance deal and get back to them.

Jan and I started to feel apprehensive about the legal path. We contacted an attorney and discussed the facts. It would be a very tough road, but he was glad to take the case. He shared our attorney friend's concerns. This would be a full court press on the ER company and the hospital. There would be no turning back; my time working in this small city would likely be over. So Jan and I thought about it some more. We discussed it during our daily workouts; we discussed it over dinner at night—the pros, the cons. Were we doing the right thing? We couldn't let them treat us like this, could we? Should we be happy with the severance? How many times in your life are you paid to not work?

A week or so later, I received a certified letter. It was from the ER company. They had terminated me, as they had threatened, and since I didn't agree to their terms, I was done. Officially, they cited my lack of compliance with the wellness committee request for an IME. Although I should have expected the letter based on the phone conversation with the ER company, I was still hurt. I had never been fired before; it was not a good feeling.

I was embarrassed to share the news with Jan. We sat and felt sorry for ourselves for a little while, but then, we propped each other up and said we would fight. That's who we were; we weren't going to let them push us around. I fired off an e-mail to the ER regional VP. I noted that I was terminated under false pretense. I had not failed to comply with the committee request. In the time prior to hearing from the committee, I certainly didn't feel I needed the IME, but once I heard there were concerns, then I certainly understood why it was requested. I still didn't think I needed it, but if there was a good reason for them to request, then I obviously would have no choice but to do it. I also noted that with the help of the hospital administrator, we found a clinic in Albuquerque that could see me in three months. So the ER company had not given me the opportunity to comply; they fired me before I ever had the opportunity to obtain an evaluation.

It was also around this time that I sent them a longer e-mail, a synopsis of how I felt they had wronged me from being misled about becoming the ER director to being told I wouldn't get that position via a single line text to being the last of a number of Hispanic and Spanish-speaking doctors to be pushed out of the ER group and be replaced largely by white males in a community that was a minority-majority city in a minority-majority state. And finally, in the ultimate slap in the face, they promised my job would be waiting for me when I contacted them after my MI, and now they were firing me for having an MI. I let them have it.

When I told my lawyer friend of the e-mail, he wasn't excited. *Well,* I thought, *what did I have to lose at this point?* They needed to all be made aware of where I stood and how I had been treated. Who knew how much the dishonest ER director had shared with ER regional VP? At the very least, at this point, they knew my point of view and what I experienced, whether they cared to know or not.

I must have struck a chord. The ER company replied and indicated they would be glad to give me another opportunity to sign a severance deal. It was the most money they could offer, but if I signed, they would also provide me with impeccable letters of recommendation and they would be happy to help me with any new job opportunities I might find. Hmm, that is weird that they reoffered and lightly sweetened the deal *after* they gave me a deadline and fired me.

Jan and I discussed what this might have meant. We talked to our lawyer friends. Yes, we had probably exposed them, but was it worth what we would have to sacrifice in the end? We called the employment attorney again, his partner, who would end up handling the details of the case talked us through the process. He painstakingly discussed the details and offered, this would not be an easy road; in fact, he specifically said that he wouldn't want anyone in his family to go through it. He noted that the ER company would make our life hell, and it was possible and likely we'd end up somewhere close to what has already been offered, minus the attorney's fee. He wasn't discouraging us per se; he was just being honest. His financial gain was dependent on what he could negotiate for us or win for us in court. He was being real. This was not a million-dollar case; there should be no visions of grandeur. As our lawyer friend had pointed out weeks ago, large corporate entities are not in business to just write you check when they are sued. They would use their vast resources to do all they could to make sure I was seen as unworthy of any payout. In addition, during the pandemic, all legal cases were taking much longer than normal to get heard. This would likely take years.

As was typical, Jan and I sat and discussed. We prayed. We sat and calculated finances. We ultimately decided we would sign the deal; more than anything, we wanted closure on this aspect of our lives, and we wanted to be able to move on. The severance pay would give us a nice cushion for a few more months and good letters of recommendation would be critical if I was to find work again in the region. We called the attorney back, notifying him. He was gracious and understood. He offered his help if needed in the future. I contacted the ER company, requesting that the money be paid by the end of the month. It was November; the holidays were near.

It was time to fly to Dallas. It was race day. We arrived in Dallas after a short flight from El Paso. We had booked a nice, fancy family suite in a boutique hotel in downtown Dallas. It was large and had multiple bedrooms and a large table, at which we could all gather and share a meal to celebrate our race and Thanksgiving. After checking in, Jan and I slipped on our running gear. It was late afternoon in Dallas; the weather was a perfect, sunny, and calm at fifty-five degrees Fahrenheit.

Jan had fashioned me a T-shirt to wear. I had the idea for the T-shirt in my mind for a few months now. It was a gray Nike Dri-FIT T-shirt, upon which Jan had ironed on "DEAD to 5K." We caught a couple of people doing double takes on our way out the door. We stretched and tried to warm up some, then Jan started our official time on her Apple watch, and off we ran up to McKinney avenue, then we crossed the street and ran through the Crescent Hotel parking lot. There were always great cars in the parking lot there: Rolls-Royce, Porsche, Bentley—all very cool.

We found a smaller street to head west on toward the American Airlines Arena. We jogged to then around the arena. We checked in with each other; both of us felt great and continued our faster than normal pace. We went up to and across the street in front of the arena then behind the W Hotel. We then went south toward the House of Blues. We were doing great! The pace was good; we were doing so much better than we expected. The lower elevation provided us with a much higher partial pressure of oxygen. It felt great! We surpassed our usual splits. We walked intermittently, as we had planned, but with the excitement, we ran much more than we ever had. We turned around and ran back through victory park and around the arena once more and back toward McKinney to our hotel. On the return trip, we took more time to enjoy and celebrate our run. We stopped briefly for selfies that we would later share with friends and many of those who had been involved with my care along the way.

The time flew by. We ran to the very end! We did it! Jan and I hugged and squelched any tears. We were not going to be sad! We were going to smile brightly and scream our triumph loudly. We had been through so much; this was our victory stand! We took more selfies and individual pics; we started to send to family and friends while we cooled down outside in the courtyard. Fortuitously, just about this time, Shelby drove up! She had been on her way to celebrate the completion of the 5K with us! What a perfect day! We made our way upstairs and, along with Luke and Anna, opened the champagne. I was restored!

CHAPTER 12

JOB SEARCH

We celebrated Thanksgiving in Dallas and had a wonderful time; we truly took the time to be grateful. It was our best premeal prayer ever, and the fact that we were able to all be together was all the more pleasing. We sat in the wine room of the Dragonfly restaurant at Hotel ZaZa. Uh-oh! They had bottomless mimosas. What a great Thanksgiving it would be.

We made it back home to Las Cruces and really got to work trying to find me work. Jan had been trying to return to work during all of this time, but with the pandemic, there weren't many opportunities. I started in earnest contacting physician recruiting services. I contacted all the local hospital recruiters. I was willing to do anything: emergency room work, primary clinic work, even wound care. At this point, I just needed to get a solid full-time position. Christmas was nearing, and I wanted to have a job or at least plans for a job before the New Year.

The whole discussion with recruiters was painful. As with most aspects of medicine, there is a hierarchy. In emergency medicine, the hierarchy involves being emergency medicine trained and boarded, which seems intuitive, but there are many primary care physicians who have chosen to pursue careers in emergency medicine, most of whom have had the same or largely overlapping training experiences. In addition, those that aren't emergency medicine trained are typically required to have years of experience working in emergency rooms, which is typically only allowed after an initial time of training or supervised work.

I switched specialties in residency after a huge disruption—a revolt, actually—occurred in the neurosurgery program I was in and rendered it ineffective. I was the lone resident left behind after the dust had settled, not because of any personal commitment to the university on my part but because I was the youngest resident, and the revolt had occurred primarily during my intern year. By the time I completed my intern year and got to my neurosurgery post, the senior residents had all moved to other programs in a coordinated effort aimed at showing support to our department chairman, who had been demoted and ultimately left the program. I had no idea such things happened in neurosurgery residency programs, but it was not the first time it happened at UNM and later, I would find, at other small programs in the country.

So I made the very painful decision to find a more stable line of work. I requested and was allowed to move into the internal medicine residency program, which was headed by a very kind and welcoming residency director, Dr. Gately. Along the way, I had decided I would complete my training and move back to my hometown, Lovington, to start my practice as a general medicine primary care clinic doctor. In order to do so, I would be required to work in the ER, as the docs in Lovington took turns covering the ER. So I beefed up my ER training and spent time training in the main ED and pediatric ED at UNM before I completed my residency. I enjoyed it. Well, I didn't really enjoy the pediatric ED; does anyone?

While in Lovington, I did my requisite clinic and hospital work; in these old medicine models, the physicians took care of every aspect of their patients' care. If they needed a clinic appointment, the physician saw the patient in clinic. If the patient needed to be admitted to the hospital, the physician would write the inpatient orders and make rounds on the patient until they were discharged. Finally, the physicians would take his turn, covering the emergency room overnight, one night during the week, and also covered one full weekend a month. So I dutifully performed all aspects of clinical medicine, but the ER was what I really enjoyed—the procedures, the heightened awareness, and emergencies. I was able to use my surgical background both in practice and in mentality. In the time since I first arrived in Lovington, the working physician model there has modernized and now has department specific physicians, as in most larger hospitals. That is to say, the clinic doctors perform the clinic work, the emergency doctors only work in the ER, etc.

After eight years in Lovington, I moved to Las Cruces to take over the urgent care medical director position. I also requested ER privileges for part-time work in addition to my full-time duties at the UC. This was the first time I encountered or even heard of—really— the idea that I wouldn't be allowed to work in the ER since I wasn't ER trained. Legally, primary-care-trained doctors with significant ER experience are allowed to work in the ER; this obviously occurred more in rural areas, as you can't expect to find a board-certified ER doc for each town. I appealed to the CEO and ER director; they agreed to give me a trial run. As the CEO would later tell me. "You blew everyone away. They love you." Ha! Board-certified ER my ass.

I found all you really need to do is treat people well, be competent, and treat your coworkers well. It helps to be pragmatic and follow the guidelines, being stern when needed; otherwise, just don't to be an asshole. It seemed to work for me, although now that I think about it, there may be a few people I worked with along the way who may take a second glance at that "don't be an asshole" line.

And so, with each recruiter, the conversation would always turn to experience and training and board certification. I was always baffled at the condescending tone of a recruiter. "Oh, you're not board-certified ER? You won't be able to work for us," they would say, or some variation of the same. It amazed me; here is someone who hasn't met me, is incapable of doing what I do, has yet to check a reference, yet was determining for an entire community what type of medical service would be available to them. They were acting like it was the premier trauma center in the country. No wonder there were so many open ER positions in so many different places.

I chuckled in particular at one experience after I e-mailed a couple of recruiters directly. They were in charge of two different ER positions in the region. I got the usual reply, asking that I confirm my training and certification. I replied with my details and waited for a response. I then heard nothing. I called to follow up after a few days; no reply. I waited a week or two and e-mailed again; no reply. Huh, was I getting ghosted? The lack of professionalism was astounding. It was no wonder towns couldn't find ER docs; the recruiters were either out playing golf or at happy hour, I supposed. I never once got a call back and told, "Thanks for your interest, but we are holding out for ER-boarded applicants." At most, it would be, "I'll check with the facility," and then no further reply.

I had the same frustrations with primary care positions. I would apply online only to have the recruiters call back. "Oh, sorry, we're looking for family-practice-trained physicians," they would say. I had all the same thoughts. I had years of primary care clinic, urgent care clinic, ER and hospitalist experience—what more could they want? *And* the position has been open for a year. Are you kidding me?

Thankfully, Lovington continued to have a need for help in their ER. Dr. Carver kindly contacted me with open shifts and allowed me to take them. It was a remarkably kind gesture and certainly one he didn't have to make. I don't know if he knew exactly how much these shifts meant to us both financially and emotionally. Because of his kindness, I was able to continue to have some income and continue to keep my mind challenged and my skills sharp.

The more time passed and the prospects of getting work locally began to whittle away, we started to consider moving. We expanded our blanket of possibilities. It was amazing to me. I had only months before been a practicing physician with multiple jobs and fighting on the frontlines during an epidemic. Now, here I was. I couldn't seem to find a good fit or anyone willing to give me a chance. I grew remarkably frustrated because I knew I was capable of helping in any ER, and my local hospital didn't want me. Meanwhile, the pandemic continued; physicians were flying in from out of state to work. How was that safer for our citizens? I didn't get it. I was continually amazed at how wild this life had become.

Almost overnight, I started to feel a little down most days. I didn't feel like working out. I did continue to work out, mostly out of fear that if I didn't, my heart would somehow worsen, but I didn't have the burning desire to do it. I noticed Jan not being her usual bubbly self either, which made me feel worse. Had I finally dragged her spirit down with all my illness and negativity? I wouldn't say I was overtly depressed. I think that would be a disservice to those who truly are depressed. I was still able to find things to enjoy, but the outlook seemed bleaker, the future more uncertain, the definite arrival of good times less likely. Maybe it was the season. To say the least, we weren't quite in the Christmas mood.

It came to a bit of a head one day. Jan and I continued to be home all day together, still following the same routine: *Today* show, check our stock option positions, exercise, lunch, nap, clean house, look for jobs, etc. One afternoon, Jan came in from another visit to the grocery store. She had tears in her eyes. "What's wrong, babe? You okay?" I asked.

"I don't know," she confessed.

"Has something happened? Do you feel okay?" I queried.

"No, I don't feel okay," Jan very bravely admitted.

I quickly went over to her and hugged her. Her tears flowed. I held mine as best I could; she didn't need a cry buddy; she needed to know we were going to be okay. The events from the morning I first went into the hospital, to the days of ICU uncertainty, to the stress of my coming home with an external defibrillator and staying awake all night most nights, to the bombshell accusations and indifference of the ER company, to the lack of professional courtesy and close-minded recruiters, to limited job prospects during a pandemic—it was all too much and was bearing down here today.

We held each other, and I confessed that I was bummed too, but I knew brighter days were ahead. I wasn't sure I fully believed it, but I desperately wanted it to be true. Maybe we could just say to hell with it. We could leave and find a small Mexican beach town, live a simple life, maybe even provide medical care to people who would might appreciate our efforts more. The thought of living a simple idyllic life by the water and a nice glass of wine seemed to brighten our mood.

In the days that followed, we slowly got better. Whether it had been the need to just let out our feelings and fears or if it was that we took any pressure off ourselves to meet a certain standard, we recovered our drive and belief in ourselves. We continued to go to church, and that provided some measure of comfort. We had good friends continuing to check on us; a couple, in particular, always seemed to provide a card at just the right time, Jim and Judy. They were an older couple we became friends with after I worked for Jim at a chemical plant before medical school in Hobbs, New Mexico. Jim and Judy were energetic and lively dinner partners, and they were wine connoisseurs, so we always enjoyed their visits to Las Cruces.

Typically, before their visits, we would gather what we thought might be good bottles of cabernet sauvignon. I would always call ahead to the restaurant we chose to be sure we could bring our own bottles. It was just easier than trying to find a restaurant we all liked or were in the mood for that also had a great wine list. It was during one of these wine rich evenings that Jim brought up the idea of me learning to fly. He had his pilot's license, and he and his wife had flown across the country. He didn't fly anymore but said he had enjoyed it. He planted the seed. Jan jumped on it and got me an introductory flight with Frost Aviation in Las Cruces for Christmas that year. Although I was a little apprehensive, I made it to the introductory flight and managed to complete it without getting sick. I also almost enjoyed it, so I was committed thereafter and earned my private pilot's license in December 2018.

Jim and Judy, like so many other friends and family, were consistent in their support of us. They sent meals, cards, and prayers. They always seemed to have a follow-up card that showed up at the right time. And so it was no surprise when another of their cards of support showed up shortly after our days of being down. It made us smile.

Jan and I made a plan. Together, we swore we would welcome in the New Year. We promised we would commit ourselves to continue and extend our exercise regimen. We would increase our cardiovascular work and start adding strengthening exercises; we would join a gym. We would be open to any work opportunities, local or not.

We suddenly had an epiphany. Why not just open our own clinic? I had experience running a clinic and being a director. We could learn the billing aspect. Jan, anxious to return to work, could get her medical assistant license, which would mean getting her back in school and something to focus on outside of keeping me healthy. It was going to be great!

CHAPTER 13

STARTING AGAIN

After the New Year, we started to put our plan in place. We joined the gym. It was the change we needed. Our workouts were reinvigorated. We got to get out of the house and see other people. We committed to improving our diet. Jan started her classes and was enjoying being in learning mode. She did not have a medical background, so it was all very exciting, eye-opening, and challenging.

As if on cue, job opportunities began to present themselves. There was a new hospital opening in town, and they needed ER docs. I applied and was hired. A local research company was looking for a doctor to serve as primary investigator on various clinical trials they would be conducting for a number of drug companies; I applied and was hired. A plasma company reached out after they reviewed my online application. An upstart house call and telemedicine company reached out; they needed a medical director. The opportunities were great and gave us more hope financially than we had in a while.

More than just the economic gains from these jobs, they also gave me a sense of worth again. In spite of my years of work experience and past successes, it was hard being asked to leave my previous ER job. The job search had been futile and so much more demeaning due to the lack of positive response. Now, though, I had the opportunity to regain my strength. We could find some semblance of a normal routine, and we could breathe a little easier. We took advantage and made plans for a nice dinner out and a top-notch bottle of wine.

It has been an amazing ride. The morning of Father's Day 2020, I woke up with chest pain that I couldn't make go away. The pain increased, and I began to vomit. I hurried and showered to go in to the ER for a quick EKG. I was hoping to put my mind at ease and be sure this wasn't cardiac. I called out to Jan, "I think I need you to call an ambulance."

"Are you sure?" she asked.

"Yes!" I confessed.

She called 911. I lay down on the couch in the living room, clutching my chest. I started sweating as I lay there in the classic clinical sign. The pain was a tight, deep, nauseating burn, and no matter what I did, I could not make it go away. I started to fear this was much more serious than I had initially thought.

Jan stood in front of me, her voice trembling, as she spoke into her phone, "Yes, I think my husband is having a heart attack," the tears streaming down her face. I will never forget this image.

When the ambulance arrived, the very kind emergency medical technicians came in; they recognized me from the ER. "Oh, hey, Doc. What's going on?" they asked, surprised to be standing in my living room.

"Oh, I'm just having a little chest pain," I replied.

By then, the pain had resolved slightly and I was able to speak comfortably. "Well, let's check your blood pressure and get a quick EKG," he said as they started to apply all of their medical equipment.

I felt the coolness of the EKG leads as they were applied in each specific position on my chest. "Hold still for us, Doc," the EMT kindly requested. How many times had I said that to a patient in the ER, hoping they could do so, so as not to cause any unwanted markings on the EKG tracing.

I heard the printing of the EKG. "Do you want to take a look at it, Doc?" he asked.

"Sure," I said as he passed me the EKG. *Shit, there were ST elevations in the anterior leads! This is not good*, I thought to myself. *I'm going to need a cardiac catheterization and likely a stent.* "Oh shit!" I said out loud.

Jan asked, "Does it look bad?"

"I'm having a heart attack, and there are changes on the EKG. I need nitro and an aspirin," I said loud enough for the EMTs to hear.

"Coming right up, Doc! Then we're heading out!" he exclaimed.

I never imagined I would ever be the patient in this scene. I was Super Dad! I was the emergency room doctor who took are of people in this scenario! I was a runner, a pilot, a golfer, and the guy always having the most fun during family gatherings. How could this be real? Maybe we would get to the ER, and this would all be nothing more than some gastroesophageal reflux and some repolarization abnormality on the EKG. God, *I could die!*

This life-changing event led me down a path I could never have guessed or dreamed. The challenges were different from any I had ever experienced before and stretched across all facets of life. I was stripped down in terms of my health, my faith, my physical strength, my mental strength, my career goals, my self-worth, my ability to perform my job, and ultimately, my resolve.

I now choose to see the positive gains this remarkable experience gave me. My family came together and is now closer and stronger than ever. We now share openly our thoughts, feelings, and concerns. There is no more facade of being Super Dad. We share responsibilities, and any physical limitations I have, I share openly and confidently. I work but don't live only to work. I enjoy taking care of people again. I look forward to a bright future and am okay with not having that future fully detailed and planned.

I stay in touch with amazing friends. I toast them with wonderful glasses of wine. We plan trips and vow to see each other as often as we can. I tell them I love them. I love hanging out with my brother and his family—in particular, my nephew, who can almost outrun me. I hug my brother every chance I get.

I paid off all my medical bills. Only a couple of the specialists turned my balances over to collection agencies. I called them to let them know how much that wasn't appreciated. I left it there. I didn't carry any anger or disappointment forward. That said, there has to be a better way to bill patients. People can't continue to be bombarded by multiple billers after they get home to recover. It is unsettling. It's unnecessary. Maybe someone will find a way.

I still don't know what the true reason the ER company had for asking me to resign. Surely, some perceived decreased stamina wouldn't be enough. Was it liability? Was it retribution for my sharing too honestly, potential changes I would make if I were made the director? I don't know. I truly don't care anymore. They paid me to not work in the midst of a pandemic—a blessing.

I still spend most of my time with Jan, but we also take time to be on our own. We continue to exercise and eat well—well, mostly. We still cherish the moments alone, drinking a glass of wine. Now, though, rather than regale her with stories of how great I used to be, we sit and speak of the amazing acts of love and support we received from friends, strangers, neighbors, and family. She continues to share stories from my time in the hospital, and I continue learning something new about the time I was gone to the world: the kindness of security guards and my man Manny, who continues to periodically text to this day, to ask how I'm doing.

Jan and I are better to each other and for each other. We don't stress over too much, even finances, and we try to see the positive in all circumstances; it isn't always easy. We still hold on to the idea that at any moment, we might just walk away from it all and head south to walk the warm beaches of Mexico. Restored.

> And the God of all grace, who called you to his eternal glory in Christ, after you have suffered a little while, will himself RESTORE you and make you strong, firm and steadfast. (1 Peter 5:10, NIV; emphasis mine)

EPILOGUE

THANK YOU

ER nurses: I send my heartfelt thanks to the amazing nurses and techs who were on duty the day I came in. I have had the opportunity to speak to most of them and thank them in person. Although mentioned briefly in the body of this story, the truth is the nurses and techs worked on me in full resuscitative efforts for well over an hour. When many would have rightfully stopped all efforts, they believed, they persisted, they made it be. They saved me.

Many nurses, in particular the ER and ICU nurse managers, came in on their day off to help save me. When I was stabilized long enough to go to the cath lab, a group of nurses came together in the now-empty ER trauma room and lifted me up in prayer. They saved me. I have been able to see and talk to Joanna, Candis, and Erika. I remain forever grateful to you and the many others involved.

ICU nurses: The ICU nurses were involved two-fold. A couple responded to my code blue call in the ER. I know or have heard a couple were also a part of the prayer group in the ER: Josh, Ryan, Kat, Julie, Adrianna. I can't thank you enough for watching over me during the most treacherous first days. I apologize to you all for my delirium and craziness and for likely saying things that I, to this day, have no idea that I said. A warm lunch and a card can't adequately express how much it meant to me that you not only saved me but that you were a comfort to my wife and kids. I hope you are all blessed sevenfold.

Doctors: I thank my colleagues who were placed in such an unenviable position. I won't try to list everyone for fear of overlooking someone. I must specifically thank Dr. Ponce, my cardiologist, who dealt with my cardiovascular instability like the true badass she is. I thank her for the extra effort and for caring. I also would like to thank Dr. Banda, who served as my ICU doc and ultimately discharged me from the hospital; your confident and kind care were critical in helping me to find my strength during remarkably scary times. Dr. M., my emergency room colleague, I'm sorry our first meeting was so dramatic; I thank you for being well trained and for making the trip to New Mexico.

Security guards: The whole group of security guards showed up in what was supposed to be a role of keeping everyone distant in the time of COVID. Your presence turned into so many of you going up to Jan and the kids and sharing kind words about me and what I meant to you. You offered your prayers and support. This display of kindness was witnessed and shared by multiple family members. The head of security, Manny, fighting his own medical battle, made sure my family was taken care of the day I arrived in the ER, and he continues to reach out in support long after. Blessings to you all.

Las Cruces work colleagues: In spite of administration not reaching out, there were so many colleagues: Shawn, Cameron, Barbara, Michael, and Val from the ER. Waterman, who also checked in with Jan and helped lend medical advice during my ICU stay. Cindy and Cynthia, Brian, Sam, Kara, Missy, Dr. Rivera Candace, Shannon, Lori, Liz, Norma, and Candace from the urgent care clinics. I thank you for the prayers, cards, texts and meals. I read so many names and wonderful declarations of support from most, if not all of the staff in the UC and ER.

Prayer warriors: It just so happens some of the greatest prayer warriors that exist are a part of my family. Perhaps that is why God found favor in me. From my mother-in-law Pat to my sisters-in-law Lisa and Melinda, I was inundated with prayers. As noted in my story, former CEOs, high school friends, childhood friends, former colleagues—all raised me up. My childhood neighbor Jimmy Crawford, now a pastor, sent may timely prayers. This kindness and support is overwhelming and emotional to me. I thank you and wish you all blessing in return.

Lovington: I mentioned briefly in the body of this story the many great friends and classmates who reached out to me. It would take an entire chapter to get through the list of individuals I heard from directly and about whom I heard had raised me up in good thoughts and prayer. My old basketball coach, Chief, was one of the first to call when I got home; my old work colleagues and first mentors in medicine Drs. Hopkins, Homer, and Carver. My old teammate Petimo. I appreciate your kind words of support and good thoughts. Chad, thanks for looking out for me so that I could remain employed. Former teaching colleagues Loran, Big Dog, Hill, and Johnny Mo Moore; high school friends Brennan Murphy, Lance clayton, Lisa Leal Gomez, Pam Dunlap Quinones, and the many other high school friends who posted on the alumni site online. I received all your good wishes. I was moved by your words and your sharing of thoughts and prayers. The friends at Nor-Lea General Hospital, from the new friends I made while working there recently to the old friends and coworkers from my previous stint, I thank you for your kindness and support.

Las Cruces: So many friends and neighbors reached out during and after my hospital stay. It has been difficult during COVID to see everyone face-to-face, but please know that your many cards, meals, texts were all appreciated. My man Jeremiah, who has always been a solid pillar of support, along with his family, I look forward to sharing good times again soon. Our friends at Sonic, who always checked on Jan and asked about me during her drive through visits for a soda.

Jim and Judy: I may have actually understated the magnitude of your support in the body of this story. I thank you. Your kind and supportive words, cards, and prayers were such a comfort, and the brotherly advice was appreciated. I can't wait for the day we get to raise a glass together again.

Family: So many texts and calls and visits. Mom and Dad, Aunt Lisa and Uncle Joe continuing to text for wellness checks. My nieces Amanda and Katy, my nephew Ethan, your love and support are heartwarming and comforting. On a grander scale, the love and support of family have been a great example to the next generation as we all grow older together.

Joe: My buddy and confidant. I thank you for supporting Jan and the kids with your candor and medical insight. I, as always, appreciate your friendship and the fact that you're always available to lend a hand. Of course, it was your encouragement that got me to learn stock option trading that was a true lifeline during the uncertain economic times. You're a rock star; keep swinging it like boom boom.

Jess and Sky: You both showed up within hours of finding out; you stayed to make sure the family was okay. I was not surprised to hear about all you did. You can't imagine how proud I am to have friends like you. I can't thank you enough for all your support and love and for finally letting me meet Jan! Love you.

Ike: I've spent most of my life trying to live up to what a big brother should be. Yet in my time of need, it was my little bro who, after Jan called, was the first to arrive. Thanks for joining Jan and the kids for the noon conference calls with the doctors while I was in the hospital, and thank you for helping me live such a great life. Thanks mostly for helping Ethan send me get well videos.

Shelby, Luke, and Annalise: I was so proud of all of you for stepping up in the time of need. I hope that long before you read this, you know how much I love you and how much I believe in you. I couldn't have asked for a finer crew. You shone during the dark days, and your love and kind words, cards, and big signs are forever etched in my brain. I love you.

Jan: I am certain there are no words that could encompass the magnitude of what you mean to me. From the late-night visits to the hospital because I couldn't rest to taking command of the medical conference calls, I hope by the sheer number of "Jan and I" starts to sentences in this story, it is evident to you and to everyone how critical you were to my survival and my recovery. I thank you for each note slipped into my car on the way to a job interview, to my first day of work, to my last day of cardiac rehab. You are truly the warmth and the sunshine.

ABOUT THE AUTHOR

Dr. Acosta is a physician and entrepreneur. *Restored* was born from his efforts to prepare a memory box of his experience suffering a near-fatal heart attack for his family. Dr. Acosta found that, in writing his thoughts and memories for his family, a remarkable and compelling story arose. *Restored* is his first published manuscript.

Dr. Acosta is a former teacher, coach, oil field chemist from Southeastern New Mexico. He is a rusty private pilot and avid golfer. He is married and has three children.

CPSIA information can be obtained
at www.ICGtesting.com
Printed in the USA
BVHW071722221121
622226BV00001B/82